HOTSPOTS
COSTA
& COSTA DORADA

Written and updated by Nick Inman
Original photography by Nick Inman

Published by Thomas Cook Publishing
A division of Thomas Cook Tour Operations Limited.
Company registration no. 3772199 England
The Thomas Cook Business Park, Unit 9, Coningsby Road,
Peterborough PE3 8SB, United Kingdom
Email: books@thomascook.com, Tel: + 44 (0) 1733 416477
www.thomascookpublishing.com

Produced by Cambridge Publishing Management Limited
Burr Elm Court, Main Street, Caldecote CB23 7NU

ISBN: 978-1-84848-085-8

First edition © 2007 Thomas Cook Publishing
This second edition © 2009
Text © Thomas Cook Publishing
Maps © Thomas Cook Publishing/PCGraphics (UK) Limited

Series Editor: Adam Royal
Production/DTP: Steven Collins

Printed and bound in Spain by GraphyCems

Cover photography: Front: 4Corners/Gräfenhain Günter

CONTENTS

WHAT'S IN YOUR GUIDEBOOK?

Independent authors Impartial up-to-date information from our travel experts who meticulously source local knowledge.

Experience Thomas Cook's 165 years in the travel industry and guidebook publishing enriches every word with expertise you can trust.

Travel know-how Thomas Cook has thousands of staff working around the globe, all living and breathing travel.

Editors Travel-publishing professionals, pulling everything together to craft a perfect blend of words, pictures, maps and design.

You, the traveller We deliver a practical, no-nonsense approach to information, geared to how you really use it.

● *Costa Brava – the 'wild' coast*

INTRODUCTION
Getting to know the Costa Brava & Costa Dorada

Puig de
Comanegra
▲
1558

Llanca

Figueres   Roses   *Cap de Creus*
                                Cadaqués

N260
Olot   Empuries
Banyoles   L'Escala
                        L'Estartit

                        Platja de Pals

Girona   C255   Tamariu
Girona ✈   Palafrugell   Llafranc

C25

                Platja d'Aro

Lloret de Mar   Tossa de Mar
A7   Pineda
de Mar   Blanes
A19   Malgrat de Mar
Calella de la Costa

Mataró

Costa del Maresme   Costa Brava   Costa Brava

Mediterranean Sea

France
Costa Brava &
Costa Dorada
Spain

○	City
○	Large Town
○	Small Town
═══	Motorway
───	Main Road
	Minor Road
✈	Airport
	Railway

N

**Costa Brava &
Costa Dorada**
0   20 km
0   15 miles

Getting to know the Costa Brava & Costa Dorada

The names alone give you a fair idea of what to expect. The Costa Brava ('Wild Coast') is for much of its length a tortuous line of cliffs thick with woods and tangled shrubs, punctuated by attractive bays and coves. It was the first part of Spain's Mediterranean coast to receive foreign

🔺 *Miami Platja cove, Tarragona*

holidaymakers en masse in the 1950s but because of its topography has never been overdeveloped. The Costa Dorada (Costa Daurada in Catalan, or 'Golden Coast') is a more low-lying and gentle shoreline named after its long, wide, gently sloping sandy beaches. Squarely placed between the two coasts is the great seaport and dynamic cultural centre of Barcelona, which offers high-brow art and architecture, shopping and street entertainment in equal measure.

Together, the Costa Brava and Costa Dorada make up the coast of Catalonia (Catalunya), an autonomous region that runs from the Pyrenees in the north to the glassy paddy fields of the Ebro delta in the south. It is one of the largest, most sophisticated and most prosperous regions of Spain and it is defined by more than geography and economics. The Catalans consider themselves a nation within a nation, with their own history, traditions, literature and cuisine. Above all, they have their own language, Catalan, which, like Spanish and French, is derived from Latin. This is used everywhere for place names and street signs and for many people it's their first and most familiar language, although they will usually be happy to switch to Spanish or English if this facilitates communication.

There are some good reasons for going to Catalonia instead of heading for the mega-resorts of the Costa Blanca and the Costa del Sol. The climate offers plenty of days of sunshine and comfortable daily summer temperatures in the high 20s °C (70s °F) without the stifling heat and breezeless days further south. The sea is generally warm and safe for swimming and all kinds of watersports, and the beaches are equipped with good facilities. The restaurants of Catalonia, meanwhile, are renowned for their fish and seafood, and the region produces an abundance of good red and white wines as well as *cava*, Spain's version of champagne.

When you have had enough of sand and sea and food and drink, you'll find there is plenty more to do. The resorts offer a broad spectrum of outdoor and indoor activities and nightlife, and there are some great excursions to be made to delightful cliff-top gardens, inland and coastal nature reserves, ancient monasteries and medieval towns.

THE BEST OF COSTA BRAVA & COSTA DORADA

If you want to do more than flop on the beach, both the Costa Brava and the Costa Dorada offer a brilliant range of things to see and do. You'll find one of Spain's best theme parks and two exciting cities only a step away, while short excursions will take you through picturesque countryside to fascinating towns, abbeys, monasteries and museums.

TOP 10 ATTRACTIONS

- **Scenery** The Costa Brava is at its most scenic between Tossa de Mar and Sant Feliu de Guíxols, and between Calella de Palafrugell and Begur. Drive the coast road or take a speedboat excursion calling into all the little coves.

- **Tarragona** The old Roman capital of the Western Mediterranean is filled with ancient monuments, including a seaside amphitheatre (see page 84).

- **Monasteries** For a superb day out visit Montserrat, a mountainside complex reached by cable car or rack railway (see page 73), or the peaceful royal mausoleum of Poblet (see page 89).

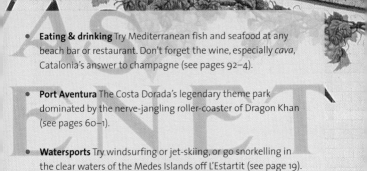

- **Eating & drinking** Try Mediterranean fish and seafood at any beach bar or restaurant. Don't forget the wine, especially *cava*, Catalonia's answer to champagne (see pages 92–4).

- **Port Aventura** The Costa Dorada's legendary theme park dominated by the nerve-jangling roller-coaster of Dragon Khan (see pages 60–1).

- **Watersports** Try windsurfing or jet-skiing, or go snorkelling in the clear waters of the Medes Islands off L'Estartit (see page 19).

- **Barcelona** Spend at least a day in the Catalan capital absorbing its art, street-life and especially the bizarre architecture of Antoni Gaudí (see page 77).

- **Nightlife** At its best in the larger resorts of Salou, Sitges and Lloret de Mar, but best of all in Barcelona.

- **Fiestas** here involve fire-breathing monsters and teams of daredevil acrobats who build human towers (see page 106).

- **Salvador Dalí** The world-famous Surrealist artist came from Figueres, where he left a wildly eccentric museum (see page 71).

◆ *The Freixenet cava bodega, Sant Sadurní d'Anoia*

SYMBOLS KEY

The following symbols are used throughout this book:

ⓐ address ☎ telephone ⊕ fax ⓦ website address ⓔ email

🕓 opening times ⓪ public transport connections ❶ important

The following symbols are used on the maps:

🏚 information office		O	city
✉ post office		O	large town
🛍 shopping		○	small town
✈ airport		■	POI (point of interest)
✚ hospital		═	motorway
🚓 police station		—	main road
🚌 bus station		⋯	minor road
🚆 railway station		—	railway
Ⓜ metro			
✝ church			

❶ numbers denote featured cafés, restaurants and evening venues

RESTAURANT CATEGORIES

The symbol after the name of each restaurant listed in this guide indicates the price of a typical three-course meal without drinks for one person:

£ = under €20 **££** = €20–€40 **£££** = over €40

▶ *Fishing boats pulled up on the beach at Calella de Palafrugell*

Roses

Situated apart from the other resorts of the Costa Brava, Roses stands on its own bay at the northern end of the Golf de Roses (Gulf of Roses). Its beaches are sheltered and suitable for watersports, and when you have had enough of sunbathing and swimming it makes a handy base for excursions to such places as the delightful Cadaqués, the Dalí museum in Figueres (see pages 71–2) and even – if the mood takes you – over the French border 40 km (24 miles) north.

BEACHES

The main beach, running south from the town centre, is **Platja de Roses** (with **Platja de la Punta** next to the harbour), which continues as **Platja de Santa Margarida**. Together these beaches make up an arc of 3 km (2 miles) of sand. On the other side of the harbour is **Platja dels Palangrers**, which is popular with the residents of Roses. Moving out of town in the same direction (east) you come to the larger but not too developed **Platja de Canyelles Petites** and **Platja de l'Almadrava**, each contained in a small, semi-built-up bay. If you want a cove with fewer people and don't mind fewer or no facilities, continue in the same direction around the headlands to find beaches such as **Cala Montjoi**, **Cala Jòncols**, **Cala Calitjàs**, **La Pelosa Calis**, **Canadell**, **Cala Rostella** and **Cala Murtra**. Out of season, if you're lucky, you may get one of these little beaches to yourself.

THINGS TO SEE & DO

Aquabrava

This waterpark has one of the biggest wave pools in Europe, as well as a few dry attractions.

ⓐ Carretera de Cadaqués, La Garriga ⓣ 972 254 344
ⓦ www.aquabrava.com ⓛ 10.00–19.00 June–Sept
ⓝ Bus: free shuttle from Roses bus station ⓘ Admission charge

Cadaqués

This picturesque fishing village is worth visiting in its own right but many visitors come because of its Dalí connection. The artist's house in adjacent Port Lligat is open to visitors and is an easy walk from Cadaqués. Dalí and his wife constructed a labyrinth out of a few fishermen's houses. Several rooms are on show including the studio, all exactly the same as they were when the artist was in residence. The road beyond Cadaqués takes you to the bleak promontory of Cap de Creus, a nature reserve and Spain's most easterly point.

Dalí house 🕒 09.30–21.00 Tues–Sun June–Sept; 10.30–18.00 Tues–Sun Oct–May ❶ Admission charge. Call ahead to book a time

Castelló d'Empúries & Empuriabrava

While the former is an old seigneurial town of cobbled streets and mansions, the latter is the opposite – a modern marina-resort built around a network of canals that is fast becoming the nightlife capital of the Gulf of Roses. Both are worth a stroll around and they make an agreeable contrast.

Ciutadella de Roses

A Renaissance fortification containing remains of the Greek city of Rhode, founded in 776 BC, and also the ruins of the 11th-century Romanesque monastery of Santa Maria.
ⓐ Avinguda de Roses ☎ 972 151 466 🅦 www.roses.cat 🕒 10.00–20.00 (summer, 21.00 in July & Aug); 10.00–18.00 (winter) ❶ Admission charge

Sant Pere de Rodes

A Benedictine monastery on a mountainside with magnificent views over the sea. Get there by a winding road up from El Port de la Selva, north of Roses.
ⓐ Camí del Monestir, El Port de la Selva ☎ 972 387 559
🅦 www.mhcat.net 🕒 10.00–20.00 Tues–Sun June–Sept; 10.00–17.30 Tues–Sun Oct–May ❶ Admission charge

◆ *The pretty town of Cadaqués*

Skydive Empuriabrava Sector Aeroclub
Empuriabrava is Spain's parachute-jumping capital and if the fancy takes you, you can jump in tandem with a trained instructor from 4,000 m (13,000 ft), experiencing one long minute of free fall. It all gets recorded on film so that you'll have a DVD to take home with you.
ⓐ Empuriabrava ❶ 972 450 111 ⓦ www.skydiveempuriabrava.com

TAKING A BREAK

Restaurants
Cala Joncols ££ A hotel-restaurant in an incomparable setting on an unspoilt bay 14 km (8¹/₂ miles) from Roses (the last few kilometres are not surfaced). Fresh fish, seafood (particularly lobster) and rice dishes are the specialities. A children's menu is available and every Friday night there's a barbecue. ⓐ Cala Joncols, on the old road from Roses to Cadaqués ❶ 972 253 970

El Bulli £££ Make sure you book months in advance if you want a table in what has been voted 'the world's best restaurant'. It has three Michelin stars. ⓐ Cala Montjoi Ferran Adrià, Roses ❶ 972 150 457 ⓦ www.elbulli.com ❶ Apr–Sept ❶ Bookings open mid-Jan

AFTER DARK

Pacha Empuriabrava A recent addition to the Ibiza club chain.
ⓐ Empuriabrava ❶ 972 453 255

Viva A dance club which claims to be for all ages. ⓐ Sector Puigmal 7-B, Empuriabrava ❶ 972 456 000

L'Estartit & L'Escala

Separated by 10 km (6 miles) of rocky shoreline, these two small but growing resorts have a range of good beaches between them, but, more than that, they are departure points for excursions to see some of the best underwater wildlife that the coasts of Spain have to offer. Both places grew up as fishing villages and L'Escala is still renowned for its anchovies. If your tastes are for things cultural and historical, meanwhile, just outside L'Escala is one of Spain's most important archaeological sites, the Greco-Roman settlement of Empúries.

BEACHES

Both resorts have sandy beaches and shallow waters good for swimming. L'Estartit has effectively one long sandy beach accessed from the town, with a small one beside the harbour as a handy refuge on windy days. L'Escala offers more choices. The longest beach here is **Platja de Riells**, a fine-sand beach close to the town centre with lifeguard supervision and full facilities. There are other good (but unsupervised) beaches heading north out of town: **Platja del Rec**, **Platja de les Muscleres** (adjacent to the Empúries archaeological site) and **Platja del Moll Grec**.

THINGS TO SEE & DO

Empúries

Dating from the Bronze Age, this coastal settlement passed into the hands of Greek traders and in the 1st century was transformed into a Roman city. It was one of the most important ports of the Mediterranean but gradually lost its importance and was abandoned in the 3rd century.

During the last century, excavations were begun and are ongoing, with much still to be uncovered. However, several large houses with paintings and mosaics can be seen as well as public buildings such as temples, an amphitheatre, the market and Roman military camp.

Admission includes entry to the site's archaeological museum.

ⓐ Sant Marti d'Empúries (northern outskirts of L'Escala) ❶ 972 770 208
ⓦ http://ftp.mac.es ❻ 10.00–18.00 Oct–May; 10.00–20.00 June–Sept
❶ Admission charge

Snorkelling off the Medes Isles

A plunge in the clear, fish-filled waters of Spain's foremost underwater nature reserve can be the highlight of a holiday on the Costa Brava. **Medaqua** will provide you with all the necessary equipment, ferry you out to a suitable spot (the location depends on the sea conditions) and tell you what creatures you are likely to see. If you are up for a bigger challenge, they'll even take you snorkelling at night. Alternatively, you can hire a kayak and snorkelling equipment from them and do your own thing.

ⓐ Passeig Marítim 13, L'Estartit (next to the harbour) ❶ 972 752 043
ⓦ www.medaqua.com

Subaquàtic Vision

If you want to see the underwater world without getting wet, this company runs three vessels (a single-hull, catamaran and trimaran) with underwater viewing cabins. You won't get as close to the fish as you would in a wetsuit but you'll certainly see things in more comfort.

ⓐ Passeig Marítim 23, L'Estartit ❶ 972 751 489
ⓦ www.cabinasubmarina.wordpress.com

TAKING A BREAK

Bars & cafés

Can Falet £ An excellent range of tapas and meals is served on the shady terrace of this bar-restaurant in a backstreet behind the harbour.
ⓐ Carrer de les Illes 33, L'Estartit ❶ 972 750 605

Port Blau £ Trendy beach-front tapas bar with a good range of sandwiches and salads. Stays open late in summer. ⓐ Passeig Marítim 13, L'Estartit ❶ 972 751 930

Restaurants
Ca La Neus ££ The restaurant of Hotel Nieves Mar on the seafront.
Fish and seafood. ⓐ Passeig Marítim 8, L'Escala ⓣ 972 770 300
ⓦ www.nievesmar.com

Les Salines ££ Fish and seafood restaurant with a view of the Medes
Islands from its terrace. ⓐ Passeig Molinet 5, L'Estartit ⓣ 972 751 611

La Gaviota £££ The place to go for a special night out in L'Estartit.
Traditional *suquets* and all manner of exquisite seafood and fish dishes
are on the menu. ⓐ Passeig Marítim 92, L'Estartit ⓣ 972 752 019
ⓦ www.restaurantlagaviota.com

AFTER DARK

Blaunit A lively bar with a dance floor and DJ. It specialises in *chupitos*
(small shots of cocktail). ⓐ Carrer Ancora 11, La Placeta, L'Estartit
ⓔ blaunit@blaunit.com ⓛ 21.00–03.00 Mon–Sun

La Devesa de Tor A highly unusual night bar ideal for a quiet and
intimate drink. ⓐ 10 km (6 miles) southwest of L'Escala on the road
from Verges to Figueres ⓣ 972 780 623 ⓦ www.ladevesadetor.com

● *A view of the Medes Isles from L'Estartit*

Begur & Pals

There's not much to draw the crowds to the town of Begur, but its indented coastline includes some of the Costa Brava's best beaches, each concealed in an attractive cove. In neighbouring Pals the situation is reversed; its long, broad beach offers endless space but little other interest, and it is the restored medieval town centre inland that will enchant you.

BEACHES

Begur's longest beach, **Sa Riera**, is also the closest to the town and has hotels, bars, restaurants and apartments on it but it doesn't feel overdeveloped. Round a rocky corner and only reachable by foot is **Platja d'Illa Roja**, a naturist beach named after the large reddish rock that dominates it. North of these two is Begur's least interesting beach, **Platja de Racó**, which continues as **Platja de Pals**, a 3.5-km (2-mile) stretch of sand backed by dunes. It has bars, toilets, a volleyball court and an area set aside for naturism.

Going south from Sa Riera, the next major beach is the less accessible, less developed and very pretty **Sa Tuna**. Next to it and reachable on car or on foot is the even more peaceful **Aiguafreda** surrounded by rocks. Round rocky headlands further south is **Fornells** with a marina and cluster of white houses around it. A footpath from Fornells (and then steps down) leads to the undeveloped **Platja Fonda**, which has coarse dark sand. The best comes last, for **Aiguablava**, on the other side of Fornells, has been voted Catalonia's best beach. It is a pleasing bay fringed by cliffs and softened by pine trees. Its only drawback is that its reputation makes it very popular.

THINGS TO SEE & DO

Barri Vell de Pals

A stroll through the atmospheric streets of old Pals is a must. The narrow cobbled lanes and archways around the Gothic church provide enough shadow to escape the heat of midday and there are art galleries and

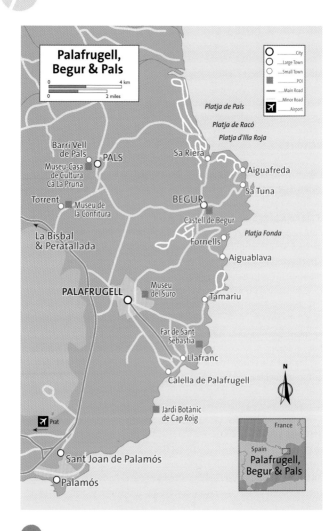

craft shops to browse in. The houses are of pretty, soft sandstone and no cars are allowed to disturb your peaceful stroll. There is a flea market here every Saturday.

Castell de Begur

A quarter of an hour's walk from Begur town centre brings you to this shell of a castle from which there are panoramic views.

La Bisbal

This pottery town has a Terracotta Museum as well as shops selling locally made ceramics. Around it are several attractive settlements including the fortified medieval town of Peratallada.

Museu-Casa de Cultura Ca La Pruna, Pals

This museum in a 15th- to 16th-century fortified house has collections of underwater archaeology and displays on Catalan winemaking.
🅐 Carrer de la Creu ☎ 972 636 833 🕐 10.30–13.30 & 18.00–21.00 Tues–Sun (summer); 10.30–13.30 & 17.00–20.00 Tues–Sun (winter)
🆆 www.pals.es ❶ Admission charge

TAKING A BREAK

Restaurants

Pizzeta £–££ Pizzas and pasta dishes are served in this small restaurant in the centre of Begur town. 🅐 Carrer Ventura Sabater 2, Begur
☎ 972 623 884 🕐 Closed Tues

Can Torrades ££ The name 'House of Toasts' tells you what the speciality is. It also serves pizzas and an assortment of grilled meats and fish.
🅐 Carrer Concepició Pi i Tató 5, Begur ☎ 972 622 881

Miramar ££ A popular place to stop for a drink, or to eat mussels or a succulent *paella*. Home-made ice creams too. 🅐 Platja de Sa Riera, Begur
☎ 972 622 228

Parador de Aiguablava £££ One of Spain's chain of luxury state-run hotels; this one is modern, on its own beautiful little pine-covered peninsula, set above Aiguablava beach. Non-residents are welcome to go in for a drink or to eat a full sit-down meal of regional cuisine. ⓐ Aiguablava ⓣ 972 622 162

AFTER DARK

Carpes de Begur Dance in the open air in this discotheque under conical awnings just outside Begur. It has two dance floors, one playing salsa and the other contemporary music. ⓐ On the road between Begur & Regencos ⓣ 972 623 745 ⓛ Every night (summer); Fri & Sat night only (winter)

● *The medieval town of Pals*

🔺 *Pretty Sa Tuna, Begur*

Palafrugell

A sense of vulnerability to attack from the sea led Palafrugell's original inhabitants to abandon their coastal settlements and found their town centre a short way inland, where it became the hub of Catalonia's cork industry. Only comparatively recently has life begun to drift the other way as the municipality discovers its other natural asset: three beautiful beaches that it has treated sensitively, allowing only low-rise, low-key development along its fringes.

BEACHES

Palafrugell's three principal beaches – **Calella de Palafrugell**, **Llafranc** and **Tamariu** – are among the most attractive on the Costa Brava. Each is set in its own small cove with a handful of restaurants and bars clustered around it. Llafranc is the most developed and Tamariu the least, whereas Calella de Palafrugell is the most appealing, with a village-like atmosphere. Off Calella de Palafrugell there are some rocky islets called **Les Formigues**. If you are feeling energetic, you can enjoy the footpaths linking all three beaches to each other.

THINGS TO SEE & DO

Far de Sant Sebastia (Sant Sebastia Lighthouse)
A steep drive or walk from Llafranc brings you to this lighthouse, one of the most powerful in the Mediterranean. You will be rewarded with an incomparable view of the thickly wooded cliffs of the Costa Blanca. Steps lead down the cliffs from the hotel above the lighthouse to a small shrine in a cave.

Jardí Botànic de Cap Roig (Cap Roig Botanical Garden)
There are magnificent views of the coast from this botanical garden where you can see thousands of exotic species. It was laid out in the 1920s by the Russian exile Nicolai Woevodsky and his English aristocratic

wife Dorothy in the grounds of their Gothic-style castle. Pretty terraces lead right down to the edge of the cliff.

ⓐ Cap Roig, Calella de Palafrugell ❶ 972 614 582
Ⓦ www.jardins.caproig.cat ❸ 09.00–20.00 (summer); 09.00–18.00 (winter) ❶ Admission charge

Museu de la Confitura (Museum of Preserves)

Learn everything you ever wanted to know about jam-making in 'the sweetest museum in the world'.

ⓐ Plaça Mayor, Torrent (4 km/2^1/$_2$ miles northwest of Palafrugell)
❶ 972 304 744 Ⓦ www.museuconfitura.com ❸ 17.00–21.00 mid-June–mid-Sept; 11.00–14.00 & 17.00–20.00 Sat, 11.00–21.00 Sun, mid-Sept to mid-June

Museu del Suro (Cork Museum)

This museum in the old town of Palafrugell explains the cork industry, important locally since the 18th century. The museum shop sells cork products. Guided tours are available.

ⓐ Carrer Tarongeta 31 ❶ 972 307 825 Ⓦ www.museudelsuro.cat
❸ 10.00–14.00 & 16.00–21.00 daily (summer); afternoons only (winter)
❶ Admission charge

TAKING A BREAK

Bars & cafés

La Croissantería de Llafranc £ The bread and croissants are made on the premises of this self-service snack bar on a square just behind Llafranc beach. It also does good takeaway salads and sandwiches.

ⓐ Plaça Promontori 11, Llafranc ❶ 972 305 152

Restaurants

Hotel Llafranc £–££ The seafood here comes daily from the fish auction at Palamós. Try, especially, the chicken with lobster or the prawns. Another house speciality is 'black rice' made with onion and tomato.

◆ *Llafranc: one of Palafrugell's popular beaches*

If you don't want a meal you can always just enjoy a drink on the terrace.
ⓐ Passeig Cypsela 16, Llafranc ⓣ 972 300 208 ⓦ www.hllafranc.com

Didal ££ Theoretically, there are almost 50 types of fish on the menu
here, what you get depends on the latest catch. ⓐ Plaça del Port Bó,
Calella de Palafrugell ⓣ 972 615 776 ⓛ Closed Mon lunch

Royal ££ This restaurant on Tamariu beach specialises in fish, seafood,
meat and rice dishes. One unusual delicacy is eels with garlic.
ⓐ Platja de Tamariu ⓣ 972 620 041

La Vela ££ You'll have a view of the beach and the rocky Formigues Isles
as you tuck into a salad, a plate of seafood or *paella*. The desserts are
home-made. ⓐ Carrer d'en Calau 4, Calella de Palafrugell ⓣ 972 616 014

El Far £££ Fish and seafood dishes are served in the stylish, light-filled
dining room of this hotel above Llafranc lighthouse. ⓐ Platja de Llafranc
ⓣ 972 301 639 ⓦ www.elfar.net

AFTER DARK

Botavara Café £–££ In the town centre, with a large selection of aperitifs
and after-dinner drinks. ⓐ Plaça del Camp d'en Prats ⓣ 972 610 154

New Arena A popular club on the old road to Calella. ⓐ Carretera Vella de
Calella, Palafrugell ⓣ 972 305 832

Platja d'Aro

A long strip of golden sand and a reputation for raucous nightlife
have made Platja d'Aro a favourite destination for both families and
partygoers. While there's plenty of entertainment on hand there's little
by way of history or culture, although there is an old town, Castell d'Aro,
a short way inland.

BEACHES

The principal beach, **Platja Gran**, is a 2-km (1-mile) extent of coarse sand.
Swimming is supervised and buoys protect the water from the approach
of motor boats. At both ends of Platja Gran the coast breaks up into
numerous coves. **Cala Rovira**, **Cala Sa Cova**, **Cala del Pi** and **Cala dels
Canyers** are all short sandy beaches to the north. **Cala Sa Conca**, to the
south, is longer and has full facilities. Beyond it is the much smaller
Cala Pedrosa.

One of the most attractive nearby beaches is **S'Agaró** at the end of
Platja de San Pol, one of the two bays belonging to the neighbouring
town of **Sant Feliu de Guíxols**.

THINGS TO SEE & DO

Aquadiver
This water park on the edge of the resort has a wave pool and an
adventure lake. You can get there on the free shuttle bus from town.
ⓐ Carretera de Circumval.lació ❶ 972 828 283 Ⓦ www.aquadiver.com
🕓 10.00–18.30 June–Sept (open until 19.00 in July & Aug)
❶ Afternoon tickets are available from 15.00 ❶ Admission charge

Castell d'Aro
The quaint old town is a handsome collection of noble stone houses built
between the 15th and 18th centuries, grouped around a Gothic church
and partially restored castle. You can drive or take a taxi to it, and the

tourist office there runs organised tours on Tuesday and Wednesday evenings in summer (winter on demand) meeting at Plaça Poeta Sitjar at 18.00.

Magic Park

Adults and children can play indoors or outdoors here. Facilities include slot machines, video games, dodgems and a bowling alley. Pequemagic is a play space for young children. UpMagic, meanwhile, is a bar with entertainment suitable for starting a night out. You might want to go on later to Club Marius, Magic Park's own discotheque.

ⓐ Avinguda Sant Feliu 86 ❶ 972 817 864 Ⓦ www.magicpark.com
❶ Admission charge

TAKING A BREAK

Bars & cafés

El Dorado Pinxtos ££ Gourmet tapas from the classic to the elaborate are served in this bar in the centre of Sant Feliu. It is one of the town's most prestigious seafood and fish restaurants. Takeaways are available in carefully packed boxes. ⓐ Rambla Vidal 17 ❶ 972 322 996

Restaurants

Cal Padú £ A popular restaurant specialising in Catalan cooking and Mediterranean fare. ⓐ B. Fanals d'Aro 71, Platja d'Aro
❶ 972 826 035

Baviera ££ This bar-restaurant and *marisquería* serves mainly seafood.
ⓐ Avenida de S'Agaró 74, Platja d'Aro ❶ 972 817 197

Hostal de la Gavina £££ There are three elegant restaurants to choose from – Garbi, Las Conchas and Candlelight – in this exclusive hotel complex surrounded by gardens. ⓐ S'Agaró ❶ 972 321 100
Ⓦ www.lagavina.com

● *The striking colours of the beach huts at S'Agaró*

La Taverna del Mar £££ A row of brightly coloured bathing huts identifies this fish and seafood restaurant on the beach of S'Agaró. ⓐ S'Agaró ⓣ 972 323 800 ⓦ www.latavernadelmar.com ⓛ Wed–Sun Oct–Apr (closed 2 weeks in Jan)

AFTER DARK

Assac Disco and bar with a novel 'stock market' pricing system for its drinks; you watch the prices on screen go up and down and buy when you are ready. ⓐ Avinguda 11 de Setembre 1 ⓣ 972 818 141

Atyco This club has four interconnected spaces offering a choice of atmospheres. ⓐ Avinguda Cavall Bernat 44 ⓣ 972 817 320 ⓛ Every night (July–Sept); weekends (Oct–June)

Discoloft A popular discotheque in Plata d'Aro organising parties on Sat nights. ⓐ Avinguda S'Agaró 120 ⓣ 972 816 379

Dicoteca Joy Another popular club. ⓐ Avinguda Pau 7, Castell-Platja d'Aro ⓣ 972 819 541

Palm Beach Club A club with three dance floors (playing techno, alternative and house, respectively) and fabulous sea views. ⓐ President Irla 15, Sant Feliu de Guíxols ⓣ 972 326 286

Tossa de Mar

If anywhere on the Catalan coast has managed to welcome tourism
without losing its charm and beauty it is Tossa de Mar, essentially a
restored medieval village commanding a beautiful horseshoe bay. Its
ancient walls climbing the slopes above the beach are one of the
picture-postcard views of the Costa Brava.

BEACHES

The main beach is **Platja Gran** which offers safe swimming in a sheltered
bay with all the facilities you would expect. **Es Codolar** is a small beach
underneath the old town; to get there, take the steps behind the
museum. **Platja de Reig** is another sandy beach not far from the town
centre. There is also good swimming and snorkelling to be had at **Platja
Mar Menuda** (also known as Sa Palma), ten minutes' walk from town.

Going south and north there are six more beaches in each direction.
To the south you will find, in the following order: **Cala Llevadó** (which has

⬤ *The beach extends from the old castle walls...*

a watersports centre), **Cala d'en Carlos**, **Cala Figuera** (naturist), **Platja de Llorell** (also good for watersports), **Porto Pi** (isolated and sandy) and **Cala Morisca** (Tossa's most unspoilt beach). North you will find: **Sant Jaume** (a pebble beach barely big enough to call itself a beach), **Cala Bona** (where the trees creep right up to the seashore), **Cala Pola**, **Cala Giverola** (which has a bar-restaurant and a few other facilities), **Futadera** (a small beach good for swimming although without lifeguard protection) and finally **Salions** (a bustling little port with a yacht marina).

THINGS TO SEE & DO

Cala Llevadó Water Sports Centre

Make the most of Tossa's clear waters by learning to water-ski, canoe, windsurf, snorkel or scuba dive here. All courses are designed for beginners; you just need to know how to swim.

ⓐ Cala Llevadó, 3 km (1³/4 miles) from Tossa ❶ 972 341 866
ⓦ www.cll-watersports.com

🔺 ...to the other end of town

Glass-bottomed boats

Take a close-up look at the seabed and peer into the sea caves between Tossa and Cala Giverola on board a glass-bottomed boat. You can get off at any of the stops and return later. Departures are from Tossa beach with the following companies:

Fondo Cristal ❶ 972 342 229 Ⓦ www.fondocristal.com ⏱ Every half hour from 10.00 June–Sept; every hour from 10.00 Apr, May & Oct

Magic Vision ❶ 972 341 624 Ⓦ www.magicvision.net ⏱ Every half hour from 10.00 June–Sept; every hour from 10.00 Apr, May & Oct

Splash Adventures

The company runs two-hour boat excursions suitable for all ages from Tossa's main beach to Cala Futadera, where you are invited to swim in the authentic 'smugglers' cave'. ❶ 628 641 890 Ⓦ www.splash-adventures.com

Vila Vella

A unique medieval Catalan walled coastal settlement built in the late 12th and early 13th centuries and reconstructed in the late 14th century, this delightful labyrinth of cobbled streets, houses and shops is the beautiful old centre of Tossa.

TAKING A BREAK

Bars & cafés

Pastisseria Tomàs £ This simple, pleasant café serves real drinking chocolate, fruit juices and teas. The cakes are home-made. ⓐ Carrer La Guardia 14 ❶ 972 340 245

Restaurants

Can Pini ££ Restaurant specialising in fish and seafood, with a wisteria-shaded terrace for summer eating. For cheaper food visit the restaurant's brasserie-pizzeria on Carrer del Tint below the town walls. ⓐ Portal 14 ❶ 972 340 297 ⏱ Closed Mon Oct–Mar

COAST ROAD NORTH FROM TOSSA
The classic corniche road squiggles its way for 23 km (14 miles) to Sant Feliu de Guixols, making for a slow but splendid drive with cliff-top views on the way.

El Portal ££ An excellent place to eat hearty fish stews and other traditional Tossa and Catalan recipes. ⓐ Carrer Pescadors 2 ⓣ 972 340 771

Tom's Steakhouse ££ English-German-run restaurant on the beach front specialising in grilled beef and pork. Children's menu available. ⓐ Avinguda Sant Raimon de Penyafort 8 ⓣ 972 341 318 ⓦ www.tomstossa.com

🔺 *The dramatic coastline near Tossa*

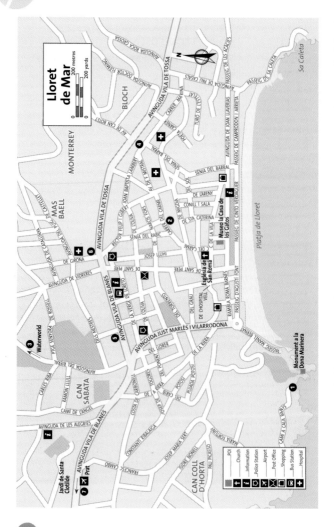

Lloret de Mar

Once a peaceful fishing village, now a byword for hair-down holiday fun, Lloret de Mar is not the place to come for peace, but if you want to spend plenty of time on the beach or dance until dawn there is nowhere better. Surprisingly, perhaps, Lloret has a long history, beginning with the founding of an Ibero-Roman trading post; the name is thought to mean 'the place of laurels'. In the 1950s it began to develop in earnest as a tourist resort.

BEACHES

Platja de Lloret is a 1.6-km (1-mile) gently sloping beach, with coarse sand and shingle. Every kind of watersport is available (parasailing, pedalos, windsurfing, water-skiing, jet-skiing, etc.) and there are most other facilities you could want, including showers, sunbeds and sunshades, first-aid points, bars and ice-cream stalls. **Sa Caleta**, a cove beneath a faux castle at the northern end of the beach, offers sheltered swimming.

The resort's second-longest beach is the **Platja de Fenals**, 1 km (1/2 mile) southwest of town, which can be reached by car or along a cliff-top path. Again, it is a sand-shingle beach and has most services you could want. If you continue past Fenals you will come to **Platja de Sa Boabella** which has few facilities, then **Platja de Santa Cristina** which has bars and restaurants, and finally, furthest away from the town, **Platja de Treumal**.

THINGS TO SEE & DO

Dofi Jet Boats

High-speed boats offering a great way to see the coast and hop between various points. The Blue Flying route connects Calella and Tossa de Mar with a stop at Lloret (first sailing 09.30) but the Blue Eye route between Lloret and Tossa (first sailing 10.00) is more interesting because it offers stopovers at almost all the coves and beaches on the way. Soft drinks and Catalan sponge cake are served on board.

📞 972 352 021 🌐 www.dofijetboats.com

Església de San Romá (San Roma Church)

Lloret's essentially 16th-century Catalan Gothic parish church has a splendidly technicolour art nouveau tiled dome and spires.

ⓐ Plaça de l'Església

Jardí de Santa Clotilde (Santa Clotilde Garden)

Romantic cliff-top gardens laid out in 1919 under the orders of the Marqués de Roviralta.

ⓐ Paratge de Santa Clotilde (between Fenals & Sa Boabella beaches)
🕐 10.00–13.00 & 16.00–20.00 Tues–Sat Apr–Oct; 10.00–17.00 Tues–Sun Nov–Mar ❶ Admission charge

Museo La Casa de los Gatos (Cats Museum)

A private collection of 6,000 exhibits strictly for cat lovers.

ⓐ Sant Albert 10 ❶ 972 366 266 ⓦ www.catsmuseum.com
🕐 10.00–13.30 & 17.00–20.00 Mon–Sat ❶ Admission charge

Waterworld

Water activities park in which the star attractions are Water Mountain, an aquatic version of a big dipper, X-treme Mountain, a 260-m (850-ft) descent in two-person rafts, and Storm, where you plummet 80 m (260 ft) and are then sucked into two large funnels by the force of the water. There are calmer pools and slides for younger children and some dry activities such as mini-golf and bungee jumping.

ⓐ Carretera de Vidreres ❶ 972 368 613 ⓦ www.waterworld.es
🕐 10.00–19.00 July & Aug; 10.00–18.30 June & Sept; 10.00–18.00 May
🚌 Free bus from Lloret's central bus station to the park ❶ Admission charge

TAKING A BREAK

Bars & cafés

Cala Banys £ ❶ It takes ten minutes to walk from Lloret to this bar on a quiet rocky inlet southwest of the main beach in the direction of Platja de Fenals. ⓐ Cami a Cala Banys ❶ 972 365 515

🔵 *The colourful roof of Església de San Romá in Lloret*

Hula-Hula ££ ❷ A bar inspired by the owners' travels in Polynesia. It specialises in cocktails, some with evocative names such as Volcano, Doctor Funk and Fog Cutter. ⓐ Carrer del Carme 36 ❶ 972 364 122 Ⓦ www.hula-hula.com

Restaurants
Mas Romeu ££ ❸ Exquisite restaurant combining seasonal ingredients, traditional dishes and a touch of innovation. ⓐ Carretera de Vidreres ❶ 972 367 963 Ⓦ www.masromeu.com

El Relicario ££ ❹ Choose between the famous flamenco floorshow upstairs (although you may have to queue to get in) or the cellar bar downstairs. Spanish and Catalan dishes. ⓐ Carrer Marina ❶ 972 365 301

AFTER DARK

Casino Lloret ❺ Play roulette, blackjack or poker into the small hours, or feed the many games machines with small change. Dress medium smart and take your passport with you. ⓐ Carrer des Esports 1 ❶ 972 366 116 Ⓦ www.casino-lloret.com ❻ 19.00–03.00 Sun–Thur, 19.00–04.00 Fri & Sat (to 05.00 in July & Aug)

Discoteca Hollywood ❻ A very popular club for tourists of all ages. ⓐ Avinguda Vila de Tossa ❶ 972 367 463

Gran Palace ££ ❼ The place for a grand night out. Dine, dance and watch the flamenco and international music show. ⓐ On the road from Lloret to Blanes ❶ 972 365 778 ❻ From 20.45

Blanes

The conspicuous rock of Sa Palomera, halfway along Blanes beach, marks the official start of the Costa Brava. The main resort with hotels, bars, apartments and restaurants is south of this point; the old town and port, reached by a delightful promenade, lie to the north. Blanes may be busy with holidaymakers in season but it is also a working fishing town with a fish auction on the return of the fleet on weekday afternoons (at around 17.00). In the last week of July, Blanes stages an international fireworks competition; a novel way to see it is from the sea on a boat excursion.

BEACHES

Blanes has five main beaches. Closest to the centre is **Platja de Blanes**, which has sunbeds and pedalos for hire. The longest beach, **Platja de S'Abanell**, is not much farther away. It has good facilities, including watersports, and is a safe place to take the family. Leaving town, the other three beaches have progressively fewer services and facilities: **Cala de Sant Francesc** (2 km/1¹/₄ miles), **Platja de Treumal** (3.5 km/2 miles) and **Platja de Santa Anna** (also 3.5 km/2 miles).

THINGS TO SEE & DO

Castell de Sant Joan
Allow an hour to climb from the harbour to this castle built from the 13th to the 16th centuries. The views from the top are worth the effort.

Catamaran Sensation
This sail-powered catamaran carries 80 passengers at a time on an excursion up the Costa Brava from Blanes port to Tossa de Mar where it moors for a while in a cove for sunbathing and snorkelling. A buffet is served on board.
🕿 627 003 307 🌐 www.catamaransensation.com 🕐 Departs at 10.00 (returns 14.00) & 14.30 (returns 18.30)

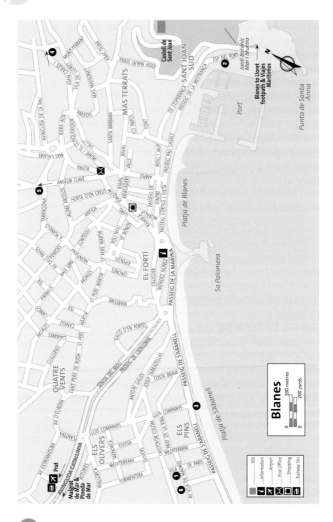

Blanes

0 200 metres
0 200 yards

POI
Information
Airport
Post Office
Shopping
Railway Stn

44

BLANES TO LLORET FOOTPATH

A section of the GR92 long-distance coastal footpath links Blanes with Lloret and passes two beautiful gardens open to the public on the way. It sets off past the Castell de Sant Joan before reaching the Pinya de Rosa Botanical Gardens, which has 100,000 specimens and one of the world's best collections of cacti. You then skirt the beaches of Treumal, Santa Cristina and Sa Boabella before having the possibility of a short detour to visit the Santa Clotilde gardens (see page 40) on the cliff top. After Platja de Fenals you can go down into Lloret where you can get a bus or boat back to your starting point. Allow two and a half hours at least to walk the 7 km (4½ miles). Ask the tourist information office in Blanes or Lloret for a map and more details.

Mar i Murtra

Escape from the crowds into these botanical gardens looking over the sea. There are over 4,000 plant species from around the world, among them cacti, herbs and palm trees. It takes an hour to follow the trail around the gardens.

ⓐ Passeig Carles Faust 9 ❶ 972 330 826
ⓦ www.jbotanicmarimurtra.org ● 09.00–18.00 April, May & Oct; 09.00–20.00 June–Sept; 10.00–17.00 Nov–Mar
Ⓝ Bus: from harbour ❶ Admission charge

Viajes Marítimos

Leave the land behind and take a boat excursion from the harbour up a scenic stretch of the Costa Brava between Blanes and Platja Aro, stopping at Lloret de Mar, Tossa de Mar and smaller places in between. There are three boats with both covered and open-air decks.

❶ 972 369 095 ● First sailing 09.40, last sailing 17.35

◔ *Fishing from the beach, Blanes*

TAKING A BREAK

Bars & cafés

Creperie Theo £ ❶   Huge choice of sweet or savoury pancakes to eat inside or at an outside table. ⓐ Avinguda Vila de Madrid 14 ❶ 372 351 080

Restaurants

Can Flores ££ ❷   One of a group of seafood restaurants next to the harbour. Relaxed and friendly. ⓐ Esplanada del Port ❶ 972 330 007

Els Pins ££ ❸   Fish and seafood on the beach. ⓐ Passeig S'Abanell ❶ 972 335 707

El Ventall £££ ❹   One of the leading restaurants in the southern Costa Brava on a hill between Blanes and Lloret de Mar. Book in advance, order a taxi and expect to pay handsomely for a good night out. ⓐ Carretera Blanes–Lloret ❶ 972 332 981 ❶ Closed Tues

AFTER DARK

La Masia de Tordera £–££ ❺   An 18th-century farmhouse a short way inland from the Costa Brava offering a Catalan dinner accompanied by a show themed around 'the Spanish night'. ⓐ Carretera de Girona, Tordera ❶ 937 650 049 ⓦ lamasiashow.com

Las Vegas ❻   Club appealing to a mainly young international crowd. ⓐ Avinguda Vila de Madrid, Els Pins ❶ 972 337 708

Costa del Maresme

A string of former fishing villages and textile-making towns makes up the resorts of the Costa del Maresme ('Marsh Coast'), which starts where Barcelona's northern suburbs peter out and ends where the Costa Brava begins. It's not the most interesting of coastlines scenically but it offers 40 km (25 miles) of sandy beaches, almost all of them with very easy access. The 'capital' of the coast is Calella but, apart from shopping, there is not much to see or do there. Busier by far is Malgrat de Mar, whose lively Passeig Marítim runs into the adjacent Santa Susanna. Pineda de Mar, between Santa Susanna and Calella, is growing and also has its share of action. Away from the beach, each of these places has an old town to explore.

BEACHES

For the most part, the beaches of the Costa del Maresme are separated from the streets of the resorts to which they belong by a coastal railway that runs along the seafront. This means that the beaches are accessible only at certain points via level crossings or underpasses. But the railway is also handy for skipping from beach to beach and even more so for a day trip to Barcelona.

Pineda de Mar beach, with its fishing boats on the sand, is particularly attractive. There are good watersports facilities at **Malgrat de Mar** and **Santa Susanna**, with pedalos, jet-skis, banana boats and sailboards available for hire. Santa Susanna also has a 'Mini Beach Club' with a bouncy castle, trampolines and slides for the little ones. Calella has a long, wide sandy beach ending in a lighthouse raised on a low headland above the sand. **Les Roques** at Calella, reached by a staircase from the main road, is a nudist beach. Two pleasant beaches in less busy parts of the Costa del Maresme are **Platja dels Pescadors** at Sant Pol de Mar and **Passeig dels Anglesos** at Caldes d'Estrac.

THINGS TO SEE & DO

Activ Natura

Swing through the trees on a high-level obstacle course using nets, cables, rope bridges and zip wires. Many other outdoor activities are also available in this family adventure playground.

ⓐ Camí de la Riera near Santa Susanna ❶ 679 443 095
ⓦ www.activ-natura.com ⓛ 09.00–20.00 July & Aug; 09.00–18.00 Sat & Sun Sept–June ❶ Admission charge

Illa Fantasia

A water park with all the classic attractions. If you don't want to make a whole day of it, half-day tickets are available from 14.00.

ⓐ Vilassar de Dalt, between Mataró and Barcelona ❶ 937 514 553
ⓦ www.illafantasia.com ⓛ 10.00–19.00 mid-June to mid-Sept ❶ Buy a combined train and park ticket and the journey is free ❶ Admission charge

Marineland

A combined zoo, dolphinarium and water park. As well as performances by dolphins, there are shows featuring sea lions, penguins and otters. The most popular attraction in the water park is the Boomerang, a vertigo-inducing fall down a slide on a float.

ⓐ Palafolls (between Blanes and Malgrat de Mar) ❶ 937 654 802
ⓦ www.marineland.es ⓛ 10.00–19.00, water park 11.00–18.30 (late April–early Oct) Ⓝ Bus: from Tossa, Lloret, Blanes, Malgrat, Santa Susanna, Pineda, Calella ❶ Admission charge

TAKING A BREAK

Bars & cafés

Casa Feliu £ Restaurant and cafeteria with long opening hours, making it as good for breakfast as for lunch or dinner. Catalan cuisine with a menu extending to 35 dishes at weekends. ⓐ Carretera NII, Santa Susanna ❶ 937 678 552 ⓛ 06.00–24.00

Restaurants

El Hogar Gallego £ Prestigious family-run seafood restaurant.
ⓐ Animas 70–73, Calella ⓣ 937 662 027

La Siesta ££–£££ An old Catalan farmhouse on a hillside outside Santa
Susanna surrounded by gardens and woods. It has a large dining room
offering dinner and Spanish variety entertainment. ⓐ Mas de Dalt, Santa
Susanna ⓣ 937 678 878 ⓦ www.masdedalt.com

⬤ *The long beach of the Costa del Maresme*

Sitges

There is still a lingering air of the sedate, well-to-do holiday town that was Sitges in the late 19th century when it was turned into a fashionable resort by the bourgeoisie of Barcelona. In their wake came artists and architects. From this period Sitges has preserved many handsome art nouveau buildings, especially the Palau Maricel, built by an American millionaire. Sitges still has an air of dignified culture but these days its attractions are more broadly based. It has a reputation for being a gay haven but is equally popular among hetero singles and couples, and families.

One thing Sitges does particularly well is celebrate. It puts on extravagant festivities for Carnival (in February or March), Corpus Christi (May or June), the *festa major* in August and the grape harvest in September. In October it hosts the world's leading international fantasy film festival.

BEACHES

Sitges has 17 sandy beaches stretching for 7 km (4¼ miles) in total. Ten of them are classed as urban beaches with easy access and safety flags. **Aquines**, **Terramar**, **Barra de la Riera Xica**, **L'Estanyol**, **Bassa Rodona**, **Ribera** and **Fragata** are effectively one beach divided up by breakwaters and connected by the Passeig Marítim. **Platja de Sant Sebastiá** and **Platja dels Balmins** on the other side of the town centre are quieter and easily overlooked. Beyond the harbour is **Platja d'Aiguadolç**, set apart from the urban beaches.

To the east of the town are four more beaches, also easy to get to and furnished with safety flags: **Cala Morisca** (naturist), **Platja de Garraf**, **Cala Ginesta** and **Platja de les Botigues** (the furthest beach from the city centre).

The remaining two beaches are west of the town and have difficult access. They are both naturist beaches. **Cala de l'Home Mort** is reached by a steep path beyond the golf course and Atlantida discotheque. A footpath from it leads to **Platja de Desenrocada**.

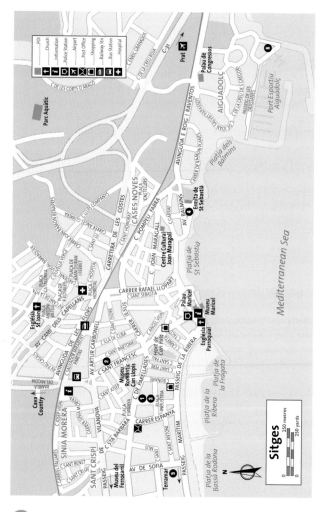

Sitges

THINGS TO SEE & DO

Cava country

Catalonia's main wine-producing region is situated inland from Sitges. *Cava*, Spain's equivalent of champagne, is made in and around Sant Sadurní d'Anoia. Several producers offer free tours and tastings. The two best-known companies are:

Codorniu ⓐ Avinguda Codorniu, Sant Sadurní d'Anoia ① 938 913 342 Ⓦ www.codorniu.es ① 09.00–17.00 Mon–Fri, 09.00–13.00 Sat & Sun

Freixenet ⓐ Joan Sala 2, St Sadurní d'Anoia ① 938 917 000 Ⓦ www.freixenet.es ① 10.00, 11.00, 12.00 & 13.00 daily

Museu del Ferrocarril (Railway Museum)

One of Spain's two principal railway museums (the other is in Madrid), it runs a steam train on the first Sunday of every month.

ⓐ Plaza Eduard Maristany, Vilanova i la Geltrú (10 km/6 miles down the coast from Sitges) ① 938 158 491 Ⓦ www.ffe.es/vilanova ① 11.00–14.00 & 17.00–20.00 (summer); closed Mon (winter) ① Admission charge

Museu Maricel

An interesting assortment of Gothic and modern art is displayed in this former hospital, which is joined to the Palau Maricel, a mansion with a lovely blue-tiled entrance patio, by a bridge over the street.

ⓐ Carrer Fonollar ① 938 940 364 ① 09.30–14.00 & 15.30–18.30 Tues–Sat (17.00–21.00 in summer), 10.00–15.00 Sun ① Admission charge

Museu Romàntic Can Llopis

The highlight of a visit to this 18th-century aristocratic house is the collection of 400 dolls displayed on the top floor. Most of them were not toys but mannequins brought back from Barcelona so that the ladies of Sitges could copy the latest fashions.

ⓐ Sant Gaudenci 1 ① 938 942 969 ① Guided tour only, 09.30–14.00 & 15.30–18.30 Tues–Sat, 10.00–15.00 Sun (17.00–21.00 in summer) ① Admission charge

TAKING A BREAK

Bars & cafés

Mont Roig Café £ ❶   This spacious café with tables in the street, an inner patio and a garden is a cool and airy place for a drink or snack. A good place for people-watching over brunch, lunch or dinner.
ⓐ Marqués de Montroig 11–13 ❶ 938 948 439 ⓦ www.montroigcafe.com

El Xatet £ ❷   One of the oldest bars in Sitges, its walls are covered with caricatures and other paintings. Tapas and sandwiches served. ⓐ Carrer Sant Francesc 1 ❶ 938 947 471

Los Vikingos ££ ❸   A busy complex with a choice of spaces to sit in, from the naturally lit patio in the middle to a gallery upstairs.
ⓐ Marqués de Montroig 7–9 ❶ 938 949 687 ⓦ www.losvikingos.com

Restaurants

El Vivero ££ ❹   If you don't believe the seafood is fresh here, ask to see the tanks of live lobsters, crabs and clams bred in the cellar, which give the restaurant its name. ⓐ Avinguda de Balmins, Platja de Sant Sebastià ❶ 938 942 149

AFTER DARK

Atlantida ❺   Sitges' largest club, open air on the seashore so that the sound of the waves competes with the music.
ⓐ Platja de les Coves, Terramar ❶ 938 949 093 ❶ Closed in winter
ⓝ Bus: from San Sebastià beach ❶ Tues nights for gay men only

Otto Zutz ❻   This off-shoot of the popular Barcelona club stands beside Sitges' marina.
ⓐ Moll de Llevant, Port d'Aiguadolç ❶ 938 944 372 ❶ From 24.00 onwards

◐ The symbol of Sitges: Sant Bartomeu church

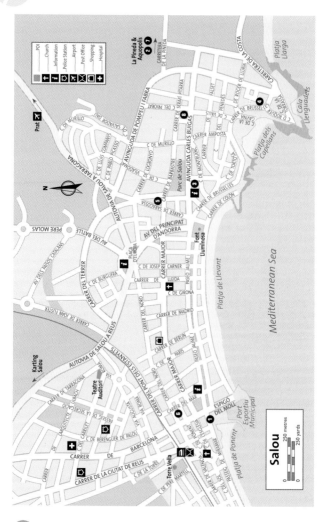

Salou & La Pineda

The Costa Dorada's favourite holiday playground, Salou, enjoyed a first wave of fashionableness in the early years of the 20th century when weekend trippers from Barcelona were drawn by its sandy beaches and briny air. It's changed since then and in recent decades has grown into one of the leading holiday centres on the Spanish Mediterranean coast. Salou is entirely geared up to a fast-paced, energetic, international lifestyle attracting both families and 20- and 30-somethings looking for a week or two partying in the sun.

Round the other side of the Cap de Salou is La Pineda, officially separate but really part of the same holiday complex. The skyline behind both resorts is dominated by the spine of Port Aventura's famous Dragon Khan roller-coaster.

BEACHES

Salou's pride is its lengthy beach divided into two by the harbour; **Platja de Ponent** to the west and **Platja de Llevant** to the east. Both sections are composed of sand running at a gentle angle into the sea, making the water safe for children. There's plenty of space for sunbathing and plenty of watersports available.

If you want to leave the crowds behind, either go west into Cambrils (see page 62) or east towards Cap Salou where there are a number of smaller beaches. **Platja dels Capellans** is urban and has a good range of services. Over a small headland is **Platja Llarga** where you begin to leave the built-up area behind. Between the two is a cove, **Cala Llenguadets**, which has to be reached on foot from Carrer de la Torrassa. At the far end of Platja Llarga are three coves: **Penya Tallada**, **Cala de la Font** (with easy access and good facilities) and **Cala Cranc** (basic facilities only). Round the other side of Cap Salou is the lengthy **Platja de La Pineda**.

THINGS TO SEE & DO

Aquopolis

Water park with two 'kamikaze' slides on which you're promised to reach 50 km/h (30 mph).

ⓐ Passeig Pau Casals 65 (on the seafront of La Pineda) ❶ 902 345 011 ⓦ www.aquopolis.es ❶ 11.00–18.00 May & Oct; 10.00–18.30 June & Sept; 10.00–19.00 July & Aug ❶ Admission charge

Font Lluminosa (Illuminated Fountain)

A fountain, spectacularly illuminated during the summer months, which was designed by the same architect as Barcelona's famous Montjuïc fountain.

ⓐ Paseo Jaume I

Karting Salou

As well as go-karts – with circuits for both adults and children (4–13 years) – this place offers trampolining, bungee rocketing, an amusement arcade and a bar.

ⓐ 2 km (1¼ miles) outside Salou on the motorway to Reus ❶ 977 385 317 ❶ 10.00–24.00 (summer); 10.00–20.00 (winter) ❶ Admission charge

Torre Vella (Old Tower)

This watchtower was built in the 16th century to give the town advance warning of pirate raids. It is now an arts centre.

ⓐ Carrer Arquebisbe Pere de Cardona 1 ❶ 977 383 235

TAKING A BREAK

Bars & cafés

Bar Gloria £ ❶ If you have a sweet tooth, this bar-cafeteria also serves thick Spanish drinking chocolate. ⓐ Passeig de Miramar 8, Salou ❶ 977 382 368

Gordon's £ ❷ A king-size breakfast and a full Sunday roast lunch are available at this bar-restaurant, which has been going since 1973. Sandwiches are also served. ⓐ Carrer Marcos Redondo 4, La Pineda ❶ 977 370 141

Tahiti £ ❸ A busy restaurant in the main shopping street serving good-value, no-frills food. ⓐ Avinguda Carles Buigas 9, Salou ❶ 977 380 339

Restaurants
Albatros ££ ❹ Salou's finest restaurant, good for a special occasion. ⓐ Carrer de Brusselles 60 (Cala Llenguadets) ❶ 977 385 070 ❶ Closed Sun night & Mon

🔺 *La Pineda beach*

Las Brasas ££ As the name ('Embers') suggests, this is the place for grilled meats. ⓐ Carrer de Barbastre 9–11 ⓣ 977 351 756

Jose Luis £££ Pricey restaurant in the Hotel Regente Aragon where you shouldn't find either the quality of the service or the food wanting. ⓐ Llevant 7 ⓣ 977 350 707 ⓛ Closed Mon & Tues

AFTER DARK

Pacha This club just back from La Pineda seafront claims to lead the Costa Dorada night scene. It has a changing programme of parties and visiting DJs. On Ladies' Night, girls get in free. ⓐ Plaça de la Cançó Catalana, La Pineda ⓣ 977 370 850 ⓦ www.pachalapineda.com

Two Much Four bars on two levels together with a terrace make up this out-of-the-ordinary nightspot where both cocktails and ice creams are served. There's always a DJ playing funk, disco, Caribbean music and oldies, and sometimes a piano player. ⓐ Avinguda Carles Buigas 37 ⓦ www.twomuch.es ⓛ 17.00–04.30

PORT AVENTURA

One of Europe's largest theme parks, Port Aventura makes a great day out for children and adults alike. It's arranged into five 'lands': Mediterrania, Polynesia, China, Mexico and the Far West, each with its own rides, shows, shops and restaurants.

Two of the rides stand out: Dragon Khan, the only roller-coaster in the world with eight loop-the-loops; and Hurakan Condor, a free-fall tower dropping you 86 m (282 ft), roughly 42 storeys.

Adjacent to the theme park is the **Caribe Aquatic Park**, a complex of swimming pools, flumes and tunnels.
ⓐ Autovia Salou/Vila-Seca ⓣ 902 202 220
ⓦ www.portaventura.es ⓛ 10.00–24.00 (summer); shorter hours (winter); Sat & Sun only Nov–Dec

AVENTURA TICKETS & TIPS

You can buy a one- or two-day pass. There is also a three-day, two-park pass covering both theme park and water park. Another option is a night pass, valid from 19.00 until closing time. Visit the website for online tickets and special deals, as well as specific opening dates and times, which change annually. Queues for rides tend to be shorter at lunchtime and in the evening.

Hold on for the Port Aventura roller-coaster

Cambrils

Other resorts must envy the way in which Cambrils manages to attract holidaymakers to its long line of fine sandy beaches without giving up its prime sources of income and community identity: agriculture and fishing. You are never far from the working fishing port where quantities of superb fish and seafood are unloaded on the docks each weekday afternoon and whisked off to nearby restaurants. Much of it is cooked using Cambrils's own Siurana olive oil which, like the best wines, has a *denominación de origen* label to guarantee its authenticity. Cambrils justifiably claims to be the 'Gourmet Capital' of the Costa Dorada.

BEACHES

Cambrils has 9 km (6 miles) of coastline divided into eight broad beaches of golden sand and calm waters protected by breakwaters and with good access and facilities. All the way along is a promenade equipped for walkers and cyclists. **Platja de L'Ardiaca**, **Platja de La Llosa** and **Platja Horta de Santa Maria** are south of the harbour. **Platja Regueral i Prat d'en Forès**, **Platja El Cavet**, **Platja de l'Esquirol**, **Platja de Vilafortuny** and **Platja de Cap de Sant Pere** are between Cambrils harbour and Salou.

THINGS TO SEE & DO

Drac Beach
This shop hires out bicycles and tandems as well as scooters, quads and electric cars. It's also a cyber café.
ⓐ Avinguda Diputació 188 ⓣ 977 354 382

Museu Agricola (Farming Museum)
A combination of museums explaining the traditional processes of olive oil- and wine-making and a shop selling local produce, particularly bottles of Cambrils' Siurana *denominación de origen* olive oil.
ⓐ Carrer Sindicat 2 ⓣ 977 360 719 ⓛ 10.00–13.30 & 17.00–20.30

Tues–Sat, 11.00–14.00 Sun, July & Aug; Sat & Sun only, Sept–June
❶ Admission charge

Museu Moli de les Tres Eras (Mill Museum)

This folk and history museum is housed in a flour mill that has been restored to working order. Among the exhibits are bronze objects found in a local excavated Roman villa.

ⓐ Via Augusta 1 ❶ 977 794 528 🕓 11.00–14.00 & 18.00–21.00 Tues–Sat (but closed Thur morning), 11.00–14.00 Sun, July & Aug; 11.00–14.00 & 17.00–20.00 Sat, 11.00–14.00 Sun, Sept–June ❶ Admission charge

Parc de Samà (Samà Park)

For a breath of fresh air away from the beach you can easily cycle or walk the 5 km (3 miles) inland to this romantic landscaped park with a lake, folly and grotto around a colonial mansion.

🕓 10.00–18.00 (winter); 10.00–20.30 (summer) ❶ Admission charge

⬥ *Fishing boats, Cambrils*

TAKING A BREAK

Restaurants
Casa Gallau ££ A classic place in Cambrils to eat choice seafood and fish.
ⓐ Pescadors 25 ☎ 977 360 261 Ⓦ www.casagallau.com 🕐 Closed Mon
night & Tues (winter)

Pósito de Pescadores ££ You may have to queue for a table in this
straightforward bar-restaurant at lunchtime, but it is worth it for the
tapas, paella and seafood. ⓐ Pescadors 23 ☎ 977 361 741

Can Bosch ££–£££ Highly rated restaurant not far from the harbour. The
cuisine draws almost entirely on local produce, the fish being landed by
the owners' childhood friends. ⓐ Rambla Jaume I 19 ☎ 977 360 019
🕐 Closed Sun night & Mon

Joan Gatell £££ Located on the harbour near the tower and offering sea
views from its terrace, this celebrated restaurant specialises in fish and
seafood. Reservation is advisable and essential at busy holiday periods.
ⓐ Passeig Miramar 26 ☎ 977 366 782 Ⓦ www.joangatell.com
🕐 Closed Sun night & Mon; 2–17 May; 15 Dec–15 Jan

Rincón de Diego £££ An elegant restaurant near Cambrils' marina.
As well as serving excellent fish and seafood it holds temporary
exhibitions by local artists. ⓐ Drassanes 7 ☎ 977 361 302
Ⓦ www.rincondediego.com 🕐 Closed Sun night & Mon

▶ *This dragon designed by Gaudi greets visitors at Parc Güell, Barcelona*

Andorra

The tiny independent state of Andorra straddles the Pyrenees between Spain and France. Most trippers going up from the coast are drawn by its sprawl of duty-free shops, although in reality these days there is not much you can buy in Andorra that you can't buy just as cheaply in a Spanish hypermarket. Beyond the shops, Andorra has attractive mountainsides spread with wildflowers, pretty villages built around Romanesque churches and, in season, splendid ski resorts.

HOW TO GET THERE

You can get to Andorra on a day-trip excursion by coach from most resorts. It's a long journey, however, and you won't get that much time in Andorra or be able to stop on the way. A better alternative is to hire a car, go at your own pace, eat at your leisure and spend a night or two in the clean mountain air.

The most direct route to Andorra from any point on the Catalan coast is the motorway from Barcelona to Manresa. Continue north to Berga and through the Túnel del Cadí to Bellver de Cerdanya. From here it's a winding mountain road west to La Seu d'Urgell, then an easy hop north into Andorra (although traffic jams can cause delays at peak times). A slower but more interesting and attractive route from the Costa Brava is across country from Girona via Besalú, Olot and Ripoll, meeting the main route north of Berga.

THINGS TO SEE & DO

The following sights are listed in the order you will reach them en route to Andorra from Girona:

Banyoles
This beautiful lake a short way northwest of Girona hosted the rowing competitions in the 1992 Barcelona Olympic Games.

⬥ *Sant Joan de Caselles, Andorra*

Besalú

A medieval town with a fortified bridge, two Romanesque churches and one of only three surviving medieval *mikvahs* (Jewish baths used for ritual bathing) in Europe.

Olot

If the peaks around here look distinctly conical it's because they are, or rather were, volcanoes.

Ribes de Freser

A delightful 1930s rack railway known as El Cremallera ('The Zip') ascends 1,000 m (3,300 ft) from here over 12.5 km (7½ miles) to a shrine and small ski-station around which there are some good walks (except in winter, of course). The road from Ribes towards Bellver de Cerdanya is very pretty but also winding enough to try any driver's patience.

Ripoll

Before Montserrat, Ripoll Abbey was the spiritual centre of Catalonia. Its portal has possibly the best Romanesque carvings in Spain.

La Seu d'Urgell

The bishop of this country town is the nominal joint head of state of Andorra along with the president of France. The only monument to stop and see is the cathedral built in the 12th century.

ANDORRA

The official language of Andorra is Catalan but everyone speaks Spanish and French, and many people also speak English. If you go on an organised tour you probably won't see more than the shopping centres in and around the country's only town, Andorra la Vella, but if you have your own transport drive north out of this conurbation towards France (or better, up the Ordino Valley) and you'll appreciate that most of the territory is forest, meadow and steep mountainside. In every village there's at least one restaurant serving local venison, wild boar or river trout. If you want to extend the excursion, drive all the way through Andorra going over a 2,407-m (7,900-ft) pass and leaving through Pas de la Casa ski resort. In France, turn right towards Latour de Carol and cross the border back into Spain between Bourg-Madame and Puigcerdá. Follow the signs for Túnel del Cadí and you will be heading back towards Barcelona.

⬥ *Cable car can be the best transport here*

Girona & Figueres

Girona, the provincial capital for the Costa Brava, has a fabulous, restored medieval town around its cathedral. It's perfect for getting enjoyably lost in but also has its fair share of modern bars and clubs if you want a night out. Its smaller neighbour to the north, Figueres, receives almost as many visitors but they only go to see one thing; the unique museum that is a memorial to the crazy talents of the Surrealist artist Salvador Dalí.

THINGS TO SEE & DO IN GIRONA

Call Jueu (Jewish Quarter)
Girona had a strong Jewish community from 890 until 1492 when all the Jews in Spain were summarily expelled. The quarter where they lived, later a ghetto, centres around the street of Carrer de la Força where Girona's last synagogue has been turned into a fascinating museum in their memory.

Museu d'Historia dels Jueus (Jewish History Museum), Centre Bonastruc Ça Porta ❷ Carrer de la Força 8 ☏ 972 216 761 🕐 10.00–20.00 (summer); 10.00–19.00 (winter) 🛈 Admission charge

Rambla de la Llibertat
The old marketplace at the bottom of the old town is now the city's main street for shopping and bar hopping. The names of the surrounding streets recall medieval trade guilds. Walk on to one of the bridges at either end for a view of the brightly painted late medieval houses that line the bank of the River Onyar.

TAKING A BREAK IN GIRONA

Bars & cafés
Artoal £ Primarily a cake shop (*pasteleria*) but also a café with an air of refinement. ❷ Pujada del Pont de Pedra 1 ☏ 972 486 046

Restaurants

El Pou del Call ££ A Catalan restaurant in the old town which does a good-value lunch menu with ample choice. There are Catalan dishes and occasionally Jewish ones. ⓐ Carrer de la Força 14 ⓣ 972 223 774

El Celler de Can Roca £££ Try this restaurant if you want to eat in the best place in the city. Run by the grandchildren of the founders, it has earned many awards, including two Michelin stars. ⓐ Carretera de Taialá 40 ⓣ 972 222 157 ⓦ www.elcellerdecanroca.com ⓒ Closed Sun & Mon

AFTER DARK

La Sala del Cel A club that claims to have introduced techno music to Spain. It has a varied programme with live bands, shows and DJs. ⓐ Carrer Pedret 118 ⓣ 972 214 664

Platea Eclectic-minded café-bar-cum-concert hall in the former Teatre Albeniz (built in 1929), which offers a variety of acts both Spanish and international. ⓐ Carrer Jeroni Real de Fontclara 4 ⓣ 972 227 288

THINGS TO SEE & DO IN FIGUERES

Teatre-Museu Dalí (Dalí Theatre Museum)

Salvador Dalí himself set up the foundation that promotes his life, work and self-proclaimed genius and runs this theatre in his birthplace of Figueres. Even if you don't much care for modern art or Surrealism, it is hard to resist the playfulness and eccentricity of it.

Be prepared for a few double takes. For instance, there's the famous pink sofa modelled on the lips of Mae West and the portrait of Gala (Dalí's companion and muse), which becomes a picture of Abraham Lincoln when seen from a distance of 18 m (59 ft).

Dalí also produced more conventional work in his earlier years. *Self-Portrait with L'Humanité* (1923) is a tentative statement of his Communist sympathies, and *Galarina* shows Gala with sensitivity.

However, it is the Surrealism that dominates. In *Soft Self-Portrait with Grilled Bacon*, painted in 1941, reality is clearly ceasing to be of much interest to Dalí and the world is turning into a weird dream – always, however, painted with an impeccable eye for light and detail.

ⓐ Plaça Gala-Salvador Dalí 5 ❶ 972 677 500 ⓦ www.salvador-dali.org
🕙 09.00–20.00 July–Sept; 10.30–18.00 Tues–Sun Oct–June
❶ Admission charge

TAKING A BREAK IN FIGUERES

Restaurants
Durán £££ Dalí often ate in this venerable old hotel restaurant founded in 1855. It still serves regional Empordanesa cuisine depending on seasonal availability. ⓐ Carrer Lasauca 5 ❶ 972 501 250

● *This could only be the Dalí museum*

Montserrat

Few monasteries in the world have such a magnificent site as this one, the spiritual heart of Catalonia, pressed to the upper slopes of the 'serrated mountain' above the plain of Llobregat. It was built in this spot, according to legend, because a statue of the Virgin Mary was hidden here from the Moorish invaders of Spain and rediscovered by shepherds in the 9th century. The local bishop ordered the statue to be moved down to Manresa where more people could see it more easily, but it became too heavy for the bearers to carry and they were forced to leave it at Montserrat. And there it has stayed since, placed in a position of honour with a Benedictine monastery and complex of other buildings gathered protectively around it.

Despite its mountain setting, Montserrat receives enormous numbers of visitors, both the faithful and the merely curious. You can get there by road or by train and there's plenty to see to fill the best part of a day. A modern block serves as restaurant, self-service cafeteria and picnic area when you need a break from spiritual sightseeing.

HOW TO GET THERE

Road Montserrat is 40 km (25 miles) northwest of Barcelona off the main road to Manresa.

Rail Take the hourly FGC train (Line R5) from Plaça de Espanya station in Barcelona. Get off either at Montserrat-Aeri station and take the cable car up the mountain or at Monistrol de Montserrat and take the rack railway. You can buy a combined train/rack railway or train/cable car ticket. ❶ 932 051 515 ⓦ www.fgc.cat

Aeri de Montserrat It takes only five minutes to get to the monastery by this cable car which has been running since 1930. ❶ 932 377 156 ⓦ www.aeridemontserrat.com

Cremallera de Montserrat This modern rack railway with air-conditioned carriages takes 15 minutes to cover the 5 km (3 miles) up to the monastery.

① 902 312 020 **Ⓦ** www.cremallerademontserrat.com

MONTSERRAT VISITA CARD

Depending what you want to see and do, it might be worth investing in this all-in-one card, which includes a ride on the rack railway or cable car, entrance to Montserrat Museum, an audioguide, a discount on the funicular railways and lunch in the self-service cafeteria.

① 938 777 701 **Ⓦ** www.montserratvisita.com
ⓔ reserves@larsa-montserrat.com

THINGS TO SEE & DO

Basilica & Sanctuary of the Virgin

Most visitors go to Montserrat to pay their respects to the statue of the Virgin, patroness of Catalonia, who is housed in her own chapel of the monastery church. She has dark skin for which she is known affectionately as La Moreneta. The monastery's boys' choir school – the oldest in Europe – performs sacred music daily in the basilica.
Basilica ⓛ 07.30–20.00 **❶** Visitors are asked to be respectfully quiet during the many services during the day
Sanctuary of the Virgin ⓛ 08.00–10.30 & 12.00–18.30

Funicular railways

The **Funicular de la Santa Cova** runs down the mountainside every 20 minutes to the Holy Grotto where the statue of the Virgin was discovered. Going in the other direction, the **Funicular de Sant Joan** goes up the mountain to a top station at 1,000 m (3,300 ft), where there is an exhibition about the wildlife of Montserrat.

◒ *The 'serrated' mountains above Montserrat monastery*

Museu de Montserrat (Montserrat Museum)

Part of this museum is dedicated to iconography of the Virgin of Montserrat but there is also an interesting collection of archaeological finds from the Middle East and a collection of 19th- and 20th-century paintings including works by the French Impressionists, Picasso and Salvador Dalí.

🕾 938 777 777 🕒 10.00–19.00 ❶ Admission charge

Sant Miquel Viewpoint

For the best view of Montserrat, follow the footpath to this platform on top of a ridge half an hour's walk from the monastery.

◓ *Vertiginous views from the cable car at Montserrat*

Barcelona

Trend-setting, energetic, enterprising, cosmopolitan, the capital of Catalonia is a must-see if you are holidaying anywhere on the Costa Brava or Costa Dorada. Although it is big, it is easy to get into from the north or south and to get around. It is packed with sights, shops, bars, restaurants and entertainment, so it helps to plan ahead and prioritise the places you really want to see. In particular, the city is famous for its Modernista architecture, a home-grown brand of art nouveau, especially the extraordinary creations of Antoni Gaudí.

THINGS TO SEE & DO

L'Aquarium

Meet sharks face to face as you walk along an 80-m (262-ft) underwater tunnel through one of Spain's largest aquariums. You'll also see manta rays, octopuses, sunfish, sea horses and a tank full of poisonous fish.
ⓐ Moll d'Espanya del Port Vell (beside Maremagnum) ❶ 932 217 474
Ⓦ www.aquariumbcn.com ❺ 09.30–23.00 July & Aug; 09.30–21.00 Sept–June Ⓝ Metro: Drassanes or Barceloneta ❶ Admission charge

Barri Gòtic

Barcelona's old town or 'Gothic Quarter' is a superbly preserved warren of medieval streets and buildings around the cathedral. It's easy to get lost but the area is not very big and you'll soon emerge on Las Ramblas or another main street.
Ⓝ Metro: Jaume I

Gaudí buildings

What distinguishes Barcelona from all other cities is the extraordinary architecture of Antoni Gaudí. His as yet unfinished, fantastically ambitious masterpiece is the church of the Sagrada Familia, but the best introductions to his work, and easiest to get to, are the cute and whimsical Casa Batlló or the magnificent, wave-like Casa Milà.

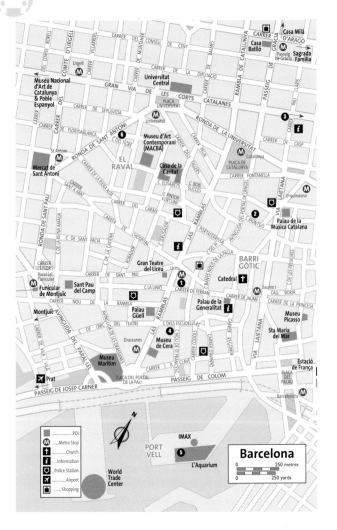

GETTING AROUND

The Metro The six lines of the Barcelona Metro interconnect with the suburban rail network (FFCC) and with the main Spanish rail network (RENFE). The air-conditioned trains provide a fast way to get around the city underground. Buy a flat-fare ticket for a single journey, a strip of ten tickets, or a one-, two- or three-day pass for unlimited use of the metro and buses. Everything is explained in English on Barcelona's public transport website (ⓦ www.tmb.net).

Bus Turístic These special buses shuttle along three routes connecting all the major sights with 44 stops. You can buy a one- or two-day ticket (adult or child) on the bus itself or in tourist information offices and get on and off as many times as you like. Your ticket entitles you to discounts (usually 10 or 20 per cent) on admission to many sights. The best place to start either route is the Plaça de Catalunya, from where buses depart every 20 minutes between 09.00 and 19.30. ⓦ www.busturistic.net

Barcelona Card These two- or three-day cards (adult and child) sold by tourist information offices give you unlimited use of the public transport system and free or very reduced (up to 50 per cent) admission to many of the city's best tourist attractions. ⓦ www.barcelonacard.com

Casa Batlló ⓐ Passeig de Gràcia 43 ⓣ 934 160 306 ⓦ www.casabatllo.es ⓛ 09.00–20.00 Ⓜ Metro: Passeig de Gracia ❶ Admission charge
Casa Milà (La Pedrera) ⓐ Passeig de Gracià 92 ⓣ 934 845 900 ⓛ 10.00–20.00 Ⓜ Metro: Passeig de Gràcia or Diagonal ❶ Admission charge
Sagrada Familia ⓐ Provença 450 ⓣ 932 073 031 ⓦ www.sagradafamilia.org ⓛ 09.00–20.00 Apr–Sept; 09.00–18.00 Oct–Mar Ⓜ Metro: Sagrada Familia ❶ Admission charge

Montjuïc

This low hill overlooking Barcelona from the south was the principal site of the 1992 Olympic Games and has several cultural and tourist attractions. It can be reached by funicular railway from Paral.lel metro station or by a spectacular cable-car ride across the port. Montjuïc's most serious monument is the beautiful **Museu Nacional d'Art de Catalunya**, a museum of Romanesque art, but anyone with children in tow is likely to head for the **Poble Espanyol**, a whole 'village' built of all the architectural styles of Spain and livened up by craft studios, bars, shops, street entertainment and activities for children.

Museu Nacional d'Art de Catalunya ⓐ Palau Nacional ⓣ 936 220 360 ⓦ www.mnac.es ⓛ 10.00–19.00 Tues–Sat, 10.00–14.30 Sun ⓘ Admission charge but free on first Sun of the month

Poble Espanyol ⓐ Avinguda Marquès de Comillas ⓣ 935 086 330 ⓦ www.poble-espanyol.com ⓛ 09.00–20.00 Mon–Thur, 09.00–04.00 Fri & Sat, 09.00–24.00 Sun ⓘ Admission charge

Museu Picasso

Don't expect to see any Cubism here, as this museum housed in adjoining medieval mansions concentrates on the artist's early works; he lived in Barcelona as a teenager and a young man.

ⓐ Carrer Montcada 15 ⓣ 932 563 000 ⓦ www.museupicasso.bcn.es ⓛ 10.00–20.00 Tues–Sun Ⓜ Metro: Arc de Triomf ⓘ Admission charge

Las Ramblas

The most famous street in Spain descends towards the waterfront from the Plaça de Catalunya past mansions, the lively Boqueria market and the opera house. It's usually packed with people and buskers. Watch your bag. Look out for artist Joan Miró's circular tile mosaic set into the pavement near the Liceu metro station. Ⓜ Metro: Liceu or Drassanes

● *Las Ramblas is always entertaining*

TAKING A BREAK

Bars & cafés

Café de l'Opera ££ ❶   You don't have to be an artist or an intellectual to while away your time in this popular but sophisticated coffee house.
ⓐ Ramblas 74 ⓣ 933 177 585 ⓦ www.cafeoperabcn.com ⓝ Metro: Liceu

Els Quatre Gats ££ ❷   A pleasant place to sit and have a drink in its own right, but most people come here to catch a whiff of Picasso who used to meet his friends here. ⓐ Carrer Montsió 3 ⓣ 933 024 140
ⓝ Metro: Plaça de Catalunya

Restaurants

Can Culleretes ££ ❸   Founded in 1786, the oldest restaurant in Barcelona. Seafood and Catalan dishes are the specialities.
ⓐ Carrer Quintana 5, Barri Gòtic ⓣ 933 173 022 ⓝ Metro: Jaume I

Los Caracoles ££ ❹   A busy, traditional restaurant known for its snails (after which it is named). It is more popular with tourists than locals but is still worth a visit for the lively atmosphere. ⓐ Carrer dels Escudellers 14
ⓣ 933 023 185 ⓝ Metro: Liceu

AFTER DARK

Maremagnum ❺   A shopping centre by day, this 'village' in the port becomes an entertainment complex after dark. The many music bars and clubs include Goldeneye, on a James Bond theme, and La City, which plays house and chart music. Sunset and Spazio Martini have terraces on which to chill out. ⓐ Moll d'Espanya ⓝ Metro: Drassanes or Barceloneta

La Paloma ❻   Interiors don't come more elegant than in this 100-year-old 'palace of dance', which combines traditional dancing with clubbing.
ⓐ Carrer del Tigre 27 ⓣ 933 016 897 ⓝ Metro: Sant Antoni

◯ The enchanting Casa Batlló

Tarragona

Tarragona may look like a modern industrial city from the outside, but at heart it's still living in the glory days of ancient Rome. In the year 27 BC it was made capital of the province of Tarraconensis, thus ruling over a large chunk of the Iberian peninsula when Barcelona was still an insignificant fishing village. The roles may have since been somewhat reversed but Tarragona has been declared a UNESCO World Heritage Site for its outstanding collection of archaeological monuments. Allow half a day or a whole day for sightseeing, depending on the level of your interest in things historical.

THINGS TO SEE & DO

Amfiteatre Romà

This oval amphitheatre was built next to the sea in the 2nd century. Part of it was carved directly out of the rock. It can hold 14,000 spectators and once held gladiatorial contests and public executions. In 259 three Christian martyrs were burned alive here.

ⓐ Parc del Miracle ❶ 977 242 579 Ⓦ www.museutgn.com
🕐 09.00–21.00 Tues–Sat, 09.00–15.00 Sun (summer); 09.00–17.00 Tues–Sat, 10.00–15.00 Sun (winter) ❶ Admission charge

Aqualeón

A water and drive-through safari park combined with exotic and predatory bird displays during the day.

ⓐ Finca Les Basses, Albinyana (northwest of Tarragona, inland from El Vendrell) ❶ 977 687 656 Ⓦ www.aqualeon.es 🕐 10.00–18.00 June–Sept Ⓝ Bus: Aqualeón Bus from all towns in the area ❶ Admission charge

Museu Nacional Arqueològic de Tarragona

Almost every Roman object found in the city that could be picked up and moved is on display here. The museum also administers an early Christian necropolis (on the way out of Tarragona towards Salou and Reus) and two Roman villas outside the city.

ⓐ Plaça del Rei 5 ⓣ 977 236 209 ⓦ www.mnat.es ⓛ 10.00–20.00
Tues–Sat, 10.00–14.00 Sun, June–Sept; 10.00–13.30 & 16.00–19.00
Tues–Sat, 10.00–14.00 Sun, Oct–May ❶ Admission charge

Old Town

An 'archaeological walk' follows Tarragona's Roman walls, which enclose
the oldest part of the city on three sides. The fourth side is formed by the
Plaça de la Font on which stands the city hall. Within the walls the centre
of things is the Romanesque-Gothic cathedral, but there are traces of
ancient buildings everywhere including Gothic arches marking the
medieval market place. It's not uncommon to go into a bar or restaurant
and find Roman stones in the walls. The remains of the Roman Provincial
forum (1st century) are worth seeing.

Pont de les Ferreres

You don't have to go into the city to see this, one of Tarragona's finest
Roman monuments, a magnificent aqueduct which strides across a
valley 4 km (2¹/₂ miles) north of Tarragona. There is a viewpoint on the A7
coastal motorway but to see it properly, take the N240 towards Valls.
There's another superb monument, the Arc de Berà, a triumphal arch,
beside the N340 heading north out of the city along the route of the old
Roman road of the Via Augusta.

TAKING A BREAK

Restaurants

El Tiberi £ Fixed-price, good-value, help-yourself buffet of Catalan food.
It's decorated in the style of a Catalan patio and the waitresses wear
regional clothes. ⓐ Marti d'Ardenya 5 ⓣ 977 235 403 ⓦ www.eltiberi.com
ⓛ Closed Sun night & Mon

Forti de la Reina £££ This is a beautiful restaurant with a history. It is
located in a reconstructed bastion built in 1707 by British troops during the
War of the Spanish Succession. The queen (*reina*) of the name is thought

to be Anne Stuart, queen of England. The terrace has views of the city and out to sea. The menu has seasonal, locally sourced produce, plus seafood and Catalan wines. ⓐ Passeig Marítim Rafael de Casanova ⓣ 977 244 877 ⓦ www.fortidelareina.com ⓛ Closed Sun night, Tues & Jan

AFTER DARK

Casino Tarragona Tables for American and French roulette, blackjack and poker as well as an assortment of gaming machines. There are two bars and a restaurant. ⓐ Rambla Vella 2 (in Hotel Imperial Tarraco) ⓣ 977 789 000 ⓦ www.casino-tarragona.com

⬥ Tarragona's Roman amphitheatre

From Salou & Cambrils

The easiest excursions from either Salou or Cambrils are into the Roman city of Tarragona (see pages 84–6) and to Reus, and there are local buses to both of them. For Poblet monastery and the Ebro delta you'll have to join an organised tour or, if you want to explore off route or stop where you please, hire a car.

Bonavista Market

The Costa Dorada's most popular street market opens for business every Sunday morning in the otherwise inconspicuous town of Bonavista, about 5 km (3 miles) outside Vila-Seca on the road towards Tarragona. Many package holidaymakers are ferried there on expensive excursions but there is a local bus from Cambrils and Salou which does the same journey for a fraction of the price (for information contact Autocars Plana ❶ 977 354 445 Ⓦ www.autocarsplana.com). Bonavista is mainly a fresh produce market, but it is worth visiting for the atmosphere and for the stalls selling crafts, souvenirs and imitation brand goods for which it's often possible to haggle.

Ebro Delta

An easy hour's drive south from Cambrils by either the coastal toll-motorway or the parallel N340 main road, the Costa Dorada bulges out to sea as the broad delta of the most important river of northern Spain, the Ebro (or Ebre in Catalan). As it approaches the sea, the river flows through the middle of a large area of marshes, paddy fields (where all the rice you have been eating comes from) and channels, making up the second-largest wetland in Europe after the Camargue in France. In peak migration season the total bird population of this delta region can reach 100,000, with cranes and flamingos the most conspicuous species to be seen. There are two information offices to help you visit the reserve: at Deltebre (the main town, on the river in the middle of the Delta) and next to the lagoon of l'Encanyissada. Being so flat, this is a good area to cycle round. Another possibility is a boat trip from Deltebre. Ⓦ www.deltebre.org

 Santa Maria de Poblet

Monestir de Santa Maria de Poblet

A 50-km (31-mile) drive inland from the Costa Dorada (via Reus and Montblanc) brings you to the peaceful Cistercian monastery of Poblet, set in beautiful woodland. Built in the 12th century and prosperous until the 18th century, it was all but destroyed in the 19th century. However, it has since been carefully restored and has a diminished community of monks still in residence. The church contains the tombs of the kings of Catalonia.

🅐 5 km (3 miles) southwest of L'Espluga de Francolí (on the N240 from Tarragona to Lleida) ❶ 977 870 089 Ⓦ www.poblet.cat ❸ 10.00–12.30 & 15.00–18.00 (summer); 10.00–12.30 & 15.00–16.30 (winter) ❶ Visits are by guided tour only ❶ Admission charge

Monestir de Santes Creus

A short drive inland from Reus, this 12th-century monastery can be found in the small medieval town of Montblanc. A stroll through one of the best preserved monastic sites in southern Europe is highly recommended.

🅐 Plaça Jaume el Just ❶ 977 638 329 ❸ 10.00–13.30 & 15.00–17.30 Tues–Sun (closes at 19.00 in summer) ❶ Admission charge

Prades, Montsant & the Priorat

If you want to leave the crowds behind, drive into the hills behind Reus. There's good walking in the Sierra de Prades and in the Sierra de Montsant, which rises to 1,163 m (3,815 ft) and is part of the Priorat wine- and olive oil-producing region. There aren't many sights as such, but at Scala Dei there are the well-tended ruins of a Carthusian monastery, and Escornalbou has a castle-monastery built in a strong defensive position.

Reus

You may have flown into Reus airport on your arrival and, like most visitors, never went anywhere near the centre. The town's only worth a short morning or afternoon stroll; its great advantages are that it is easy to get to by bus from Salou or Cambrils and you won't see too many

other tourists. Reus was the birthplace of Antoni Gaudí, the architect of so many extraordinary buildings in Barcelona, and while there is nothing of his handiwork to see here, there are other Modernista (art nouveau) houses. The tourist information office will supply you with a map for a half-hour walking tour around them.

Tortosa

Standing on the River Ebro before it opens out into the delta, Tortosa is an interesting small city. Here you can get a taste of typical Catalan culture for it does not yet feature in many tourists' itineraries. However, it is full of history: parts of the Roman city walls remain, the Moors conquered it, and it was a major battle site of the civil war 70 years ago. First, you will see the old cathedral, begun in the 12th century, which also has a lovely, tranquil cloister. Then, dominating the skyline, you cannot fail to miss the spectacular Arab fortress of La Zuda, perched on a cliff top. Here you can stay in grand style as it has been converted into a *parador* (a luxurious state-run hotel). It is well worth having at least a drink here to take in the stunning views.

▶ *Barcelona's Boqueria market*

Food & drink

Eating out is one of the great pleasures of a stay on Spain's Mediterranean coasts. Almost everywhere you'll be spoilt for choice of where and what to eat. Most bars and restaurants concentrate on what they know best and serve Mediterranean cuisine with its healthy emphasis on fresh fish, seafood, vegetables and olive oil in abundance. Smarter restaurants try to be creative with their contents and presentation, but don't be too sure that if you pay more you'll eat better; when the ingredients are fresh and good it is hard to beat straightforward Catalan home cooking. If the local food is not for you, you'll also find a range of international food (including British) on offer in any large resort.

EATING HOURS

Mealtimes in Spain are later than in the rest of Europe, although resorts that cater for international tourists have much more flexible hours. The main meals of the day are *esmorzar* (breakfast), *dinar* (lunch) and *sopar* (dinner). Breakfast in hotels is served between 07.30 and 10.00. Restaurants are open for lunch 14.00–16.00 and for dinner generally 21.00–23.00. At other times tapas may be available at a bar.

FISH & SEAFOOD

The majority of restaurants on the Costa Dorada and the Costa Brava specialise in dishes based on fish and seafood. You're never far away from a fishing harbour and you can be fairly sure that what you are served up comes fresh from the afternoon fish auction on the quayside. You can't go wrong ordering a selection of grilled fish or the reliable Catalan classic fish stew, *suquet de peix*. The only problem may be putting a name to what you are eating. A huge variety of fish and shellfish is served on the coasts of Catalonia and not every animal has a common English name.

MAR I MUNTANYA

If the fish and seafood of the coast are one strand of Catalan cuisine, the other is the meat-based cooking of the inland upland regions. But Catalans are most proud of their trademark crossover dishes known as *mar i muntanya* ('sea and mountain'), which mix ingredients that don't obviously belong together, such as chicken with lobster.

RICE

Rice is a common ingredient in Catalan cooking. Spain's best-known rice dish, *paella*, is, however, from neighbouring Valencia but it is served everywhere on the Costa Dorada and the Costa Brava. Authentic *paella* is made with either chicken and rabbit or fish and seafood but the most popular variety is a hybridised version in the *mar i muntanya* tradition. Whatever goes into it, a really good *paella* has to be cooked just before it is eaten or else the rice goes mushy. Don't trust any restaurant that will serve you an instant portion; choose instead one that makes you wait 20 minutes and brings the *paella* to your table fresh from the stove.

SAUCES

Spanish cooking doesn't much go in for sauces but Catalan cuisine is the exception. There is hardly a meal to be bought without *all i oli*, garlic-flavoured mayonnaise, placed on the table to accompany it. It goes especially well with grilled meats and rice dishes. Another typically Catalan sauce is *romesco*, a spicy tomato sauce typically used to enhance the flavour of fish.

TAPAS

One of the great things about eating out anywhere in Spain is its flexibility. You can always keep your hunger at bay with a selection of tapas (snacks, *tapes* in Catalan) which are available in almost every bar. Even smart restaurants often have a tapas bar attached. Tapas are by their nature small helpings but you can order a larger portion of anything you fancy by asking for a *ració*. Be warned, however, that a few of these can easily add up to the price of a full meal.

The Catalan snack *par excellence* – sometimes served as a complimentary pre-starter while you are studying the menu – is *pa amb tomàquet*, a slice of crusty bread with tomato, garlic and olive oil rubbed into it. A good portable snack is *entrepà*, a sandwich of unbuttered French bread filled with whatever you want.

VEGETARIAN

Catalonia has an exquisite range of fruits and vegetables but few restaurants offer a specifically vegetarian option among their main courses. Most, however, will be willing to make an effort and adapt a starter or a salad to your requirements.

DESSERTS

Spain is not particularly good on desserts but fresh fruit will always be an option and *flan* (crème caramel) is always on the menu. Catalonia, however, has two good local dishes to try. One is *crema catalana*, akin to crème brûlée, a thick custard with a burnt crust of sugar over it. The other is *mel i mató*, a goat's milk curd cheese sweetened with honey.

WINES & OTHER ALCOHOLIC DRINKS

Catalonia has 11 *denominación de origen* (DO) wine regions where grape varieties and production methods are controlled to ensure consistently high standards. One of the largest regions is Penédes. Smaller regions include Conca de Barberá, Alella and Pla de Bages. Wines from the rest of Spain are also widely available; La Rioja, for example, supplies red wines of a consistently high quality. Imported wines are available only in posh restaurants and they're not cheap.

In a league apart from all other Catalan wines is *cava*, sparkling white wine, which is much cheaper than Champagne but often just as good or even better. The two leading brands are Cordoniu and Freixenet.

Almost all beer (*cervesa*) served in Spanish bars is lager, but English pubs in the resorts may well attract you in with the promise of bitter served by the pint.

The commonest cocktail is *sangria* (red wine, fruit and a dash or more of some spirit), which makes a great summer drink but can be potent. Another popular drink in the summer is red wine mixed with lemonade.

> *Vi* (wine) can be *blanc* (white), *negre* (red) or *rosat* (rosé). Sweet is *dolç* and dry is *sec*.

SOFT DRINKS

Tap water everywhere is safe to drink but most people prefer bottled mineral water (*aigua*), either still (*sense gas*) or sparkling (*amb gas*). Colas and other popular international soft drinks and mixers are also everywhere. A healthy alternative is a glass of freshly squeezed orange juice (*taronjada*), which is available in most bars. In summer you'll also see some other thirst-quenching drinks around, particularly *horxata*, which looks like a milkshake but is made from a vegetable root.

COFFEE, TEA & CHOCOLATE

Spanish coffee is typically strong. Ask for *cafè sol* if you want an espresso, *cafè amb llet* for milky white coffee and *cafè tallat* for something in between – a black coffee with a shot of milk. If you don't like strong coffee order *un americano* and if you want it decaffeinated, *cafè descafeïnat*. And if you're after something cool rather than hot, ask for a *cafè con hielo*, which is a black coffee poured over ice cubes and sweetened to your taste.

Tea (*te*) is not widely drunk in Spain but any bar will give you a tea bag and a cup of hot water to steep it in. For a herb tea try *camamilla* (camomile) or *menta* (a type of mint).

A good winter drink is hot chocolate, *xocolata*, which is typically served with *churros*, sticks of doughy batter, to dunk into it.

Menu decoder

Menus are typically in Catalan but sometimes only in Spanish (given here in brackets). Smarter restaurants and restaurants in tourist resorts will probably have an English translation available.

A la brasa Barbecued
Al forn (al horno) In the oven
Albercoc (albaricoque) Apricot
Albergínes (berenjenas) Aubergines
Allioli Garlic mayonnaise
Amanida (ensalada) Salad
Anxoves (anchoas) Anchovies (L'Escala is particularly famous for them)
Arròs (arroz) Rice
Arròs negre Black rice cooked in squid ink
Bacallà (bacalao) Cod
Bolets Wild mushrooms
Boquerons Pickled anchovies
Botifarra A kind of sausage akin to black pudding
Bufats Hazelnut biscuits
Bunyols Fritters coated with sugar
Cabrito Kid
Calamar Squid
Calamars farcits Stuffed squid
Calçots Large green spring onions
Calçotada A green spring onion starter, which is the speciality of the Costa Dorada (onions are cooked over an open fire of vine cuttings and need to have their outer skins peeled off before they can be dipped into the almond, tomato and garlic sauce served with them)
Caragols (caracoles) Snails
Carquinyolls Almond biscuits
Carxofes (alcachofas) Artichokes
Cirera (cereza) Cherry
Conill (conejo) Rabbit
Escalivada A cold dish of roasted peppers and aubergines, usually a salad entrée or a side dish with meat
Escudella The Catalan version of a Spanish staple midday winter meal consisting of a hotpot in which the broth is served first followed by the meat (carn d'olla) as a separate course
Espinacs (espinacas) Spinach
Espinacs a la catalana Spinach with pine nuts and raisins
Esqueixada Salad made with salt cod
Farcit Stuffed
Fideuá Noodles cooked in fish-flavoured stock
Figa (higo) Fig
Formatge (queso) Cheese, mostly from sheep's or goat's milk (Catalonia produces a little cheese of its own but the most widely eaten variety is queso manchego from La Mancha in central Spain, which

can be mild (*semicurado*) or
mature and tasty (*curado*))

Fruita (fruta) Fruit

Fuet A kind of long thin sausage
made with dried meat

Gamba Prawn or shrimp

Gambas al ajillo Sautéed prawns

Gaspatxo (gazpacho) A chilled
vegetable soup originally from
Andalucia

Gelat (helado) Ice cream

Llangosta (langosta) Spiny lobster

Llangosta amb pollastre Lobster
with chicken

Llangosti Large prawn

Llomo Sliced pork

Llonganisa A kind of sausage

Lluç (merluza) Hake

Macedonia Fruit salad

Maduixa (fresa) Strawberry

Marisc (marisco) Seafood

Mariscada Mixed fish and
seafood platter

Mel i mató Goat's cheese eaten
with honey

Meló (melón) Melon

Menjar blanc A dessert made
from the creamed 'milk' of
squeezed almonds

Pa (pan) Bread

Pa amb tomàquet Bread rubbed
with tomato, salted and
drizzled with olive oil

Panellets Marzipan cakes with
pine nuts pressed into them

Pastisset (pastel) Cake

Patatas bravas Spicy chunks of
potato

Peix (pescado) Fish

Pernil (jamón) Cured ham

Pollastre (pollo) Chicken

Polp (pulpo) Octopus

Porc (cerdo) Pork

Postre de músics 'Musicians'
dessert', a dish of dried fruit
and mixed nuts, which was
once supposedly given to
travelling musicians

Préssec (melocotón) Peaches

Romesco A spicy sauce very
common in Catalan cooking

Rossejat Noodle (or sometimes
rice) casserole

Rovellon Wild mushrooms

Sarsuela (zarzuela) Seafood stew

Senglar (jabalí) Wild boar

Sèpia (sepia) Cuttlefish

Sèpia amb mandonguilles
Cuttlefish with meatballs

Sopa Soup

Suquet de peix Casserole of
white fish and tomatoes

Torrades Slices of toast with
various toppings

Truita (trucha) Trout (the same
word is used for omelette
(tortilla in Spanish), the most
popular form being made with
potato (de patata), although
you can order an omelette
with just about anything in it,
or with nothing in it)

Vedella (ternera) Veal

Xai (cordero) Lamb (costelles de
xai are lamb cutlets)

Xató Salad of tuna fish and salt
cod originally from Sitges,
commonly served as a starter

Xoriç Chorizo sausage with
paprika

LIFESTYLE

Shopping

Although international chain stores have an increasing presence in Spain, there are still many small, family-run, often delightfully old-fashioned shops catering for local customers. Service is often unhurried and you have to ask for what you want rather than browse at your leisure, but you'll get personal attention and good advice. All the resorts have a network of pedestrianised shopping streets, but for quick, unfussy shopping, you'll always find a hypermarket or shopping centre close by.

These days it's getting increasingly difficult to find anything to buy that isn't available elsewhere in Europe and you'll need to hunt around a little for a really good souvenir or present. Two good things to look for are traditional crafts and contemporary Spanish fashion and accessories.

Wherever you are, look out for the word *rebaixes* (*rebajas* in Spanish), which means sales. The two best times to go sales shopping are January and February, and July and August, but you'll see sales being held year-round in some places.

USEFUL SHOPPING PHRASES

	Catalan	Spanish
How much does this cost?	¿Quant costa aixo?	¿Cuánto cuesta esto?
I would like	M'agradaria	Me gustaría
Do you have?	¿Tenen?	¿Tienen?
I'm just looking	Només estic mirant	Sólo estoy mirando

BARCELONA SHOPPING

The only place in Catalonia for really serious shopping is the regional capital. The Eixample, an area of broad perpendicular and parallel streets laid out in the 19th century, is where you will find all the big names of Spanish fashion and design. The streets of the Barri Gòtic (around the cathedral) and the Born (adjacent to it) are full of small, highly specialised, often very interesting shops.

DEPARTMENT STORES & SHOPPING CENTRES

Spain's leading chain of department stores, El Corte Inglés, is a good place for general shopping under one roof. It has eight branches in Barcelona, the main one being on Plaça Catalunya, and one in Girona, in the Girocentre shopping centre (ⓐ Barcelona 106–110).

As well as imported goods, El Corte Inglés stocks many quality Spanish products at reasonable prices. Its supermarkets sell many gourmet Spanish foodstuffs and wines. It is also a convenient place to buy CDs of Spanish music (traditional or pop) and books, both about the local area and in English if you need something to read.

CRAFTS

The most common craft in Catalonia is pottery making, and some towns, noticeably La Bisbal, specialise in it. The main drawback, of course, is the weight, but you'll still find many portable items available.

Another good choice is a leather drinking bottle, a *bota*, which is made from goatskin. It may be the sort of thing you hang on your wall back home but in Spain it is used for its original purpose of carrying water or wine when walking or tending flocks in the countryside. The nicest ones are those not obviously made as tourist souvenirs. Some of the best come from the town of Gandesa.

A typical Catalan craft is the making of figures for Christmas cribs. Tortosa, in particular, is renowned for its workshops. Other crafts you may see are basketwork, lace, leather, jewellery and glass. Always ask if they have been made locally and buy directly from the craftsman or craftswoman if you can. It will be cheaper and you can be sure of the piece's authenticity.

Other 'typically Spanish' items such as guitars, flamenco dresses and castanets are from Andalucia, in the south of Spain, not Catalonia, but they still make great purchases if they are of good quality.

SHOPPING FOR FOOD & WINE

Shopping for food can be more than just a way of rustling up the ingredients for a picnic; it can be a good way to get to know the local culture and yield some great presents to take home with you. The easiest thing to do is go round the local supermarket – find one in a residential area away from the beach if you can – but it's more enterprising to get items such as bread from small specialist shops. Some tasty items come pre-packed for easy transport, such as L'Escala's canned anchovies, locally made cakes and biscuits and various types of cured meats and sausages. Olive oil is also a good souvenir but make sure it has been pressed in Catalonia. Cambrils (see page 62) has its own 'brand'.

Wine lovers will find plenty of choice on the Costa Dorada and Costa Brava. Wine and *cava* are available from supermarkets, specialist wine shops and, best of all, from the producers themselves. In most wine regions you can take a bottle along to the local grower's cooperative and get it filled up with good-quality table wine.

MARKETS

Most large towns have a permanent covered market, which consists of stalls selling fruit and vegetables, meat, spices, fish and seafood, although there are often hardware and other stalls outside it. Every town also has its street market one day a week for fresh produce and household goods, and some resorts run craft or themed fairs such as Lloret de Mar's 'medieval' market and Salou's craft fair at the Masia Catalana. Street markets are great for atmosphere and you may pick up a bargain, but keep a tight grip on your purse or wallet.

The largest street markets in the region are at Bonavista on the Costa Dorada (near Tarragona, see page 84) and at Tordera on the Costa Brava (inland from Blanes or Malgrat de Mar), both on Sunday morning.

MARKET DAYS
Monday: Blanes, Cadaqués, Salou
Tuesday: Lloret de Mar, Tarragona
Wednesday: Begur, Cambrils
Thursday: Sitges, Tossa de Mar
Friday: La Pineda
Saturday: Reus
Sunday: Bonavista, Palafrugell, Roses, Tarragona, Tordera

Children

Children are welcome everywhere in Spain and parents don't think twice about taking them wherever they go, even when they go out late at night. Don't, however, expect much in the way of special provisions. Only 'international' restaurants provide highchairs or offer children's menus, and few toilets are equipped with nappy-changing stations. There's plenty for older children to do in and around the main resorts, which have go-karts, bungee jumping, mini-golf and other amusements available, often on the edge of town. But it may be a good idea to have a few ideas for a family excursion up your sleeve.

ADVENTURE PLAYGROUNDS

La Selva de l'Aventura is a forest between Girona and Vic that will test any youngster's thirst for adventure with high-level walkways, platforms, rope ladders, nets, Tarzan swings and Tyrolean zip slides.

ⓐ Carretera Viladrau, near Arbúcies ⓦ www.selvaventura.com
ⓛ 10.00–18.00 Mar–Oct ❶ Children must be accompanied by an adult

BOATS, TRAINS & CABLE CARS

The Costa Brava is fun to navigate by boat. Either catch a stopping ferry and get on and off as you please, or take an organised excursion. Glass-bottomed boats sail from Tossa de Mar (see page 35) and L'Estartit (see page 19). Andorra (see page 68) and Montserrat (see page 73) have rack railways that chug steeply and dramatically uphill. And Barcelona and Montserrat both have spectacular cable-car rides.

TIBIDABO

Half the fun of this Barcelona amusement park on top of a hill overlooking the city is getting there by tram and funicular railway. And not too far away is the other great place to take children in Barcelona, the Pòble Espanyol (see page 80).

ⓐ Plaça del Tibidabo 3–4 ⓣ 932 117 942 ⓦ www.tibidabo.es
ⓛ 12.00–21.00 (23.00 in Aug)

WATER PARKS

There is at least one water park within reach of every resort on the two coasts, offering a variety of supervised slides ranging from the short and gentle to the terrifying. Typically, water parks also have quieter areas and infants' playgrounds, making them suitable places for a family day out.

ZOOS & AQUARIUMS

Barcelona has a large aquarium (see page 77). Dolphin shows can be seen at Marineland, between Blanes and Costa del Maresme (see page 49). And Aqualeón (see page 84) near Tarragona, meanwhile, is both a water park and a safari park.

STAYING SAFE

Long hours on the beach can be an enjoyable way for the family to spend time together, but the Mediterranean sun can be stronger than it looks and you should make sure children wear a hat and are coated with a copious quantity of powerful sunblock. The other potential hazard of a busy beach is disorientation and it's a good idea for younger children to wear identification bracelets in case they get lost in the crowds.

⬤ *Barcelona is full of street entertainers*

Sports & activities

Both the Costa Brava and the Costa Dorada have great facilities for practising a range of sports and activities on land or in the water, and they have the climate to make anything you do outdoors enjoyable. Whether you are a beginner or an expert, you're sure to find something to suit you.

CYCLING

The Costa Brava may be rugged and hilly but the Costa Dorada is mainly on the level and makes for easy cycling. Montroig del Camp, inland from Cambrils, is one of nine designated 'mountain bike centres' in Catalonia offering 100 km (60 miles) of signposted routes, and you can hire bikes there. The flattest place, however, is around the Ebro Delta (see page 87) where there are several bike hire firms.

FISHING

You'll need a licence (*llicència de pesca*) if you want to cast a line into one of Catalonia's many rivers, and the best place to get information is in a tackle shop on the spot; they will probably also help you fill out the application form. For more information contact the Federación Catalana de Pesca. ⓐ Calle Béjar 59, Barcelona ⓣ 932 893 300 ⓦ www.fcpeic.cat

GOLF

There are 39 golf courses on or within range of the Catalan coast. They are concentrated around Barcelona and on the Costa Brava with only five of them on the Costa Dorada. Most but not all are open to visiting players, although some have times set aside for members only. The Golf Spain website has full details of courses and prices. ⓦ www.golfspain.com

SKIING

Andorra and the Pyrenees in general have good skiing in winter. For more information see the Spanish Winter Sports Federation website.
ⓦ www.rfedi.es

WALKING

Catalonia has a great range of marked footpaths. The long-distance GR92 follows the whole Catalan coast taking in the best of the Costa Brava and the Costa Dorada between the French border and Ulldecona. Local tourist information offices will provide you with maps of the sections in their areas. Inland the possibilities multiply, and, if you are prepared to travel, the Pyrenees are a hiking paradise. Wherever you go, always take water with you and a hat to protect you from the sun. For more information see Ⓦ www.euro-senders.com or Ⓦ www.feec.org

WATERSPORTS

The sea offers an enormous range of possible activities. Swimming is the obvious thing to do and is generally safe, but always pay attention to warning flags.

Almost all resorts offer windsurfing, parasailing, water-skiing and jet-skiing. If you jet-ski, keep at least 50 m (55 yds) away from other jet-skiers, don't go into harbours and marinas or ski at dusk or at night, and always keep a good 200 m (220 yds) away from a bathing area.

Some parts of the Costa Brava are spectacular under water. The Medes islands off L'Estartit is the best place to go snorkelling or diving (see page 19) but there are diving centres in all resorts that will give you a taster session of scuba diving.

🔺 *Volleyball on the beach*

Festivals & events

Every village, town and city in Catalonia has its annual week-long *festa major*, normally during the summer months, to honour its patron saint or the Virgin Mary. They will also celebrate the major religious festivals of the year.

CARNAVAL

The first main fiesta of the year is *carnaval*, which falls in either February or March (depending on the date of Easter). This is an occasion for lavish costume parades. In Catalonia the carnival to see is that of Sitges.

EASTER

Easter Week sees elaborate processions of hooded penitents all over Spain. One of the most singular rituals is the Dance of Death performed by skeletal figures in Verges (near L'Estartit) on Maundy Thursday. Elsewhere passion plays are performed.

ST GEORGE'S DAY

Sant Jordi (St George), the patron saint of Catalonia (and England), is celebrated on 23 April. By tradition, Catalan men give their girlfriends a rose during the day and women give their boyfriends a book.

CORPUS CHRISTI

In May or June the streets of Sitges are laid with elaborate flower carpets for the holy procession to pass over. In Barcelona an egg is bizarrely set bobbing on the fountain in the cathedral cloister.

MIDSUMMER

The night of 23–24 June is Midsummer's Eve or the Night of St John, which is said to be alive with magic. Bonfires are set alight in many places and people form rings around them or jump over the embers for good luck.

LIFESTYLE

HUMAN TOWERS

The highlight of many fiestas on the Costa Dorada is an acrobatic display by a team of *castellers* who form themselves into human towers and 'castles' up to the height of a three-storey building. Dismantling a tower safely is given equal care. You can see them in Vilafranca del Penedés on 30 August and in Tarragona during the feast of Santa Tecla in late September.

AUTUMN FIESTAS

La Diada, 11 September, is Catalonia's 'national' day and is as much a demonstration of regional pride as a traditional fiesta. La Mercé on 24 September is the biggest fiesta in Barcelona. Its highlight is the *correfoc*, a nocturnal procession of devils and monsters spraying fire and sparks around them.

CHRISTMAS

As Christmas approaches, you'll see many cribs set up and also 'living cribs' in which real people and animals act out the Nativity. On the night of 5 January the Three Kings go in procession through many towns. Children get their main Christmas presents the next morning.

NEW YEAR

At midnight on New Year's Eve, people observe the national tradition of swallowing 12 grapes in succession – one for each stroke of the clock.

SARDANA

The Catalan dance of the *sardana* is performed everywhere on many occasions. You're often welcome to join in although it is trickier than it first appears. It is danced in a circle, with hands linked, in a series of skips and jumps.

▶ *The Spanish and Catalan flags flying in Lloret de Mar*

Accommodation

Price ratings are based on double room rate with breakfast in high season.
£ = under €50   **££** = €50–€100   **£££** = over €100

BEGUR & PALS
Aiguaclara ££ Family-run boutique hotel and restaurant in a colonial
house in the centre of town. All the rooms are individually decorated.
🅐 St Miquel 2, 17255 Begur 🅣 972 622 905 🅦 www.aiguaclara.com

BLANES
Hotel Boix-Mar £ Relaxing hotel 60 m (66 yds) back from the beach with
a shady garden, sun terrace and small swimming pool. 🅐 Enric Morera 5,
17300 Blanes 🅣 972 830 276 🅦 www.hotelboixmar.com

CAMBRILS
Hotel Princep ££ Purpose-built hotel in the port area, not far from the
beach. Air-conditioning and satellite TV in the 27 rooms. 🅐 Narcis
Monturiol 2 (Plaza de la Iglesia) 🅣 977 361 127 🅦 www.hotelprincep.com

COSTA DEL MARESME
Hotel Brisamar £ Functional modern hotel with a beach nearby and a
swimming pool. Help-yourself buffets served in the restaurant.
🅐 Doctor Bertomeu, Pineda de Mar 08397 🅦 www.hotelbrisamar.com

L'ESTARTIT & L'ESCALA
Hostal Santa Clara £ An inexpensive place to stay (or eat) in the resort,
located in the port and near the beach. 🅐 Passeig Maritime 18, 17258
L'Estartit 🅣 972 751 767 🅦 www.hostalsantaclara.com

Hostal Empúries ££ *Hostal* built in the early 20th century to
accommodate archaeologists working on the nearby excavations, now
serving holidaymakers using the beach. 🅐 Platja de Portitxol, 17130
L'Escala 🅣 972 770 207 🅦 www.hostalempuries.com

LLORET DE MAR

Husa Roger de Flor ££–£££ Handsome hotel a little way back from the beach but still with sea views. Garden, swimming pool, gym, solarium. ⓐ Turó de l'Estelat, 17310 Lloret de Mar ⓣ 972 364 800 ⓦ www.husarogerdeflor.com

PALAFRUGELL

Hotel San Roc ££–£££ Clifftop 1950s hotel with garden. Most of the 47 rooms have sea views. ⓐ Pl. Atlàntic 2, Calella de Palafrugell 17210 ⓣ 972 614 250 ⓦ www.santroc.com

PLATJA D'ARO

Hotel Planamar £ Beachside hotel in which all rooms have balconies. The restaurant has two vegetarian menus. ⓐ Passeig del Mar 82, 17250 Platja d'Aro ⓣ 972 817 177 ⓦ www.planamar.com

ROSES

Hotel Terraza ££ On the beach and close to the town centre. Some of the air-conditioned rooms have a view of the sea. ⓐ Avinguda de Rhode 34, 17480 Roses ⓣ 972 256 154 ⓦ www.hotelterraza.com

SALOU

Hotel Casablanca Playa £–££ A hotel, as its name suggests, on the beach. The 63 rooms have terraces with sea views. Facilities include a swimming pool, gardens and a garage for safe parking. ⓐ Paseo Miramar 12, 43840 Salou ⓣ 977 380 107 ⓦ www.hotelcasablancaplaya-rotonda.com

SITGES

La Santa Maria ££ A listed building on the seafront in the centre of town. The hotel has its own restaurant with a terrace looking out to sea. ⓐ Passeig de la Ribera 52, 08870 Sitges ⓣ 938 940 999 ⓦ www.lasantamaria.com

Preparing to go

GETTING THERE

Flying

In peak holiday season, a charter flight into Reus or Girona is the cheapest way to get to the Costa Dorada or the Costa Brava respectively, but you may have to arrive or depart at an antisocial hour. More convenient, and cheaper at off-peak times, are the scheduled flights operated by low-cost airlines such as **Ryanair** and **easyJet**, but the prices of flights fluctuate enormously. Surprisingly good deals can sometimes also be had from **Iberia**, the Spanish national carrier, which also has an efficient network of domestic flights within Spain, or **British Airways**.

The flight from London to Reus takes about two hours. Some transatlantic flights go directly from the USA to Barcelona but there will be more choice if you go via Madrid and change onto a domestic flight.

British Airways ❶ Spain 902 111 333; UK 0844 493 0787
Ⓦ www.britishairways.com

easyJet London Gatwick to Barcelona ❶ Spain 807 450 045; UK 0871 244 2366 Ⓦ www.easyjet.com

Iberia London Heathrow and other European airports to Barcelona
❶ Spain 902 400 500; UK 0870 609 0500 Ⓦ www.iberia.com

Ryanair London Stansted to Girona, and Stansted or Luton to Reus
❶ Spain 087 220 999; UK 0871 246 0000 Ⓦ www.ryanair.com

Many people are aware that air travel emits CO_2, which contributes to climate change. You may be interested in the possibility of lessening the environmental impact of your flight through the charity Climate Care, which offsets your CO_2 by funding environmental projects around the world. Visit Ⓦ www.climatecare.org

Driving

From any of the ports on the French side of the English Channel head first to Paris and take the motorway to Orléans. Turn off for Bourges and travel on the A75 through the Massif Central (passing Clermont-Ferrand and crossing the viaduct at Millau) to reach the south coast at Béziers.

Follow the A9 motorway along the coast south past Narbonne and Perpignan to cross the border into Spain at Le Boulou. The motorway continues as the A7. Exits before Barcelona lead to all the major Costa Brava resorts; after Barcelona there are exits for the Costa Dorada resorts.

Rail

It takes just over a day's non-stop travel to get from London to Barcelona by rail, changing in Paris. To plan a rail trip from the UK to Spain, it's best to go through an international agent such as **Rail Europe**.

ⓐ 1 Regent Street, London SW1 ⓣ 0844 848 4064
ⓦ www.raileurope.co.uk ⓝ Tube: Piccadilly Circus

Package holidays

An all-inclusive holiday with a reputable operator booked through a high-street or online travel agent or direct with the company will save you hassles and control your budget. Your operator will have a rep on hand to transfer you to the hotel and sort out any problems and will offer you various organised excursions. You can always adapt a package holiday to suit you and your family's needs, by eating out occasionally, arranging your own excursions, hiring a car for a day, etc.

TOURISM AUTHORITY

Before travelling you can obtain information from a number of different sources. All the resorts have their own websites, and for more general information about the area you are going to visit, the following resources are helpful:

Spanish Tourist Office ⓐ 79 New Cavendish Street, London W1W 6XB (to visit by appointment only); PO Box 4009, London W1A 6NB (to post your request) ⓣ 020 7486 8077 ⓔ info.londres@tourspain.es
ⓦ www.tourspain.co.uk ⓝ Tube: Oxford Circus or Great Portland Street
Catalonia information ⓦ www.catalunyaturisme.com
Costa Brava information ⓦ www.costabrava.org
Costa Dorada information ⓦ www.costadaurada.org

TRAVEL INSURANCE

Although EU citizenship gives you basic health cover in Spain (see page 121), it is advisable to take out personal travel insurance as well. This can be obtained from your travel agent, airline company or any insurance company. Make sure it gives adequate cover not only for medical expenses but also for loss or theft of possessions, personal liability and repatriation in an emergency. If you are going to Spain by car ask your insurer for a green card and check with them on the cover you will need for damage, loss or theft of the vehicle and for legal costs in the event of an accident. If you intend to hire a car, it's worth asking your insurer at home what your existing policy will cover; you may be able to avoid paying the car-hire-company extra premiums.

BEFORE YOU LEAVE

You don't need any vaccinations to visit Spain, nor do you need to take any particular precautions, although if you are taking prescription medication it is wise to take your own supply with you. Other than that, it's a good idea to pack a few obvious items such as a travelling first-aid kit, a hat and sunblock. But all important items will be available to buy locally in any Catalan holiday resort.

ENTRY FORMALITIES

Most visitors, including citizens of all EU countries, the US, Canada, Ireland, Australia and New Zealand, require only a valid passport to enter Spain. Visitors from South Africa must have a visa. There is no restriction on what items you may bring in with you as a tourist but you'll find almost everything you need locally. In Spain you are obliged by law to carry your passport (or other identification, such as a driving licence) with you at all times in case the police ask for identification. You will also need to show some ID when paying with a credit card.

MONEY

The Spanish currency is the euro. It is divided into 100 centésimos. There are coins of 1 and 2 euros and of 1, 2, 5, 10, 20 and 50 centésimos. The notes are of 5, 10, 20, 50 and 100 euros.

Banks are generally open only in the morning from around 09.00 to 13.30 Monday to Friday, but you are unlikely to need to go into one, as cash machines (ATMs) are plentiful in all resorts and cities where you can withdraw money with a credit or debit card. Credit cards are accepted for payment almost everywhere except in bars and smaller shops and restaurants. Traveller's cheques can be cashed in banks and big hotels. Personal cheques drawn from a UK bank in sterling are not accepted anywhere.

Prices are usually given with VAT (IVA in Spain) included. Visitors from non-EU countries can claim a VAT rebate on purchases over a certain limit; just ask for instructions in the shop at the time of purchase.

CLIMATE

Northeastern Spain's Mediterranean climate pretty much guarantees warm to hot sunny days for over six months of the year, but without the fierce heat common further south in Spain. Summer is April to September, with temperature highs in July and August. Winter days can be cold (but not freezing) and wet, but there are also likely to be sunny days during the colder months when it is possible to sit and have a drink outside in the middle of the day. Altitude also dictates the weather, so the higher up you get, even near the coast, the cooler it will be.

BAGGAGE ALLOWANCE

Low-cost airlines may stipulate a lower baggage limit than conventional airlines such as Iberia, but whoever you fly with you should look at the small print on your ticket carefully. Because of recent terrorist alerts, British airports have altered their policy on cabin or hand luggage and you should also check the latest rules for these with your airline before arriving at the airport.

During your stay

AIRPORTS

The biggest and busiest airport in the region is Barcelona (BCN), 12 km ($7^1/_2$ miles) southwest of the city. The best way to get into the city centre is by train to Sants mainline station or the metro interchange of Plaça de Catalunya.

If you are arriving on a package tour or a low-budget flight you will almost certainly fly into one of the other, smaller airports serving the coasts of Catalonia. Reus (REU) is 3 km (2 miles) from the city of the same name and about 6 km (4 miles) from Salou. There are buses from Reus airport to Salou, Cambrils and Barcelona. Girona-Costa Brava airport (GRO) at La Selva 12 km ($7^1/_2$ miles) from Girona city caters for the coast north of Barcelona. Regular buses link it to Barcelona, Tossa de Mar, Lloret de Mar, Roses and the resorts of the Costa del Maresme.

For information on Spanish airports see Ⓦ www.aena.es

COMMUNICATIONS

Phones

Avoid making phone calls from hotels as charges can be excessive. The simplest and cheapest way to make a call is from a phone box using a pre-paid card bought from a tobacconist's (*entanc*). A slightly more expensive alternative is a *locutorio*, a private telephone exchange where you are given a private booth and pay for the call afterwards.

If you want to use your own mobile phone you should check with your service provider first whether it works in Spain. Like most countries, Spain uses GSM technology, which means that if you are coming from some regions, including the USA and Japan, you need a tri-band handset. Even if you have a compatible handset, on some accounts the phone is 'barred' for use abroad and the 'roaming' service needs to be activated. You might also want to check what the call charges are. Another alternative becoming popular with over seas visitors is to buy a local SIM card for the duration of your stay. Don't forget to take your phone charger and a suitable adapter with you.

TELEPHONING THE COSTA BRAVA & THE COSTA DORADA

To call Spain from overseas, first dial the international access code (usually 00), then the country code for Spain (34), then the area code (93 for Barcelona, 972 for Girona/Costa Brava and 977 for Tarragona/Costa Dorada), followed by the local phone number.
❶ The area code is an integral part of the number and must be dialled even if you are phoning next door

TELEPHONING ABROAD

To make an international call from Spain, dial the international access code (00), then the country code, followed by the local area code minus the initial 0, and then the local number. Country codes are as follows:

Australia 61	Canada 1
Ireland 353	New Zealand 64
South Africa 27	UK 44
US 1	

International directory assistance ⓘ 11886.

Post

Post offices, *oficinas de correos*, are generally open from 08.00 to 14.00 Monday to Friday and 09.00 to 14.00 on Saturdays, but there's usually only one in town and you'll only need it if you are sending a parcel. If you just want stamps for postcards or letters don't bother to look for a post office; buy them in a tobacconist's (*estanc*), which is marked by a large T and the word 'Tabacos'. Post boxes are yellow. To send a telegram call
🔂 902 197 197. For more information on Spanish postal services see
Ⓦ www.correos.es

Internet cafés

Every resort on the Catalan coast has at least one cyber-café, usually not too far away from the beach.

Paris 2000 @ Falset 6, Salou ☎ 977 351 814
Sitges Café @ Verge del Pilar 12, Sitges ☎ 938 113 431
Ciberpanther @ Pg. Camprodon i Arrieta 34, Lloret de Mar ☎ 972 366 527
La Paleta @ Avinguda Costa Brava 32, Tossa de Mar ☎ 972 342 975

CUSTOMS

A little understanding of how society works in Catalonia will go a long way to getting what you want and even making friends. Although many people you meet will be from other parts of Spain, many will be native-born Catalans. As such, they may resent being called 'Spanish' and they will certainly be impressed if you show an awareness of how their history and culture differs from that of Madrid and the Costa del Sol. A large part of the population uses Catalan as its first language and if you can manage a few words of this it will be taken as a sign of respect. Spanish is also an acceptable lingua franca and English is widely spoken in the resorts.

Even if you can't master the local language, be aware that politeness and common courtesies matter greatly in Spain. Always begin any conversation, even if you are only asking for directions, with *bon dia* (*buenos días* in Spanish) in the morning or *bona tarda* (*buenas tardes*) if it's after lunch. The more informal *hola* can be used at any time of day. Likewise, when entering a shop, office or public place always say a general 'hello' to those present and don't leave without an *adéu* (*adiós*). Please (*si us plau/por favor*) and thank you (*gràcies/gracias*) are not used quite as much in Spain as they are in Britain but you certainly won't go wrong if you say them.

DRESS CODES

Catalonia is generally a tolerant and informal place and in the resorts it is taken for granted that people dress to be comfortable. But it is as well to be aware of a few unspoken rules. Spaniards tend to dress smart or ultra-casual with nothing in between. If you want to do any serious business, appearances matter greatly and you should look your best.

Few restaurants impose a dress code, but unless you're in the most laid-back beach bar, put a shirt on if you are eating a meal. It is also respectful to cover up before wandering into a church.

Topless sunbathing is tacitly accepted in most places, but if you want to strip off completely, ask for the nearest *playa nudista* (naturist beach). This is likely to be in a secluded bay a little way from the main resort.

ELECTRICITY

Spain's electricity supply is 220 volts but you may find the odd anachronistic 125-volt outlet in an older building and it's worth double-checking the voltage before plugging in a sensitive appliance like a computer or a mobile phone. Plugs in Spain have only two round pins (live and neutral but no earth), so electrical devices from the UK will need an adapter. Visitors from North America need a transformer.

EMERGENCIES

There are separate emergency numbers for the various services you may need, but one number, 112, will always get you through to what you need. All emergency numbers are listed in telephone directories under Servicios de Urgencias. For help and advice, you'll always find a police office close to the local town hall or you can ask inside the town hall for assistance.

Another useful organisation to contact in case of trouble is the Spanish Red Cross, which maintains fleets of ambulances and lifeboats, and has trained paramedics stationed on the busiest beaches.

📞 902 222 292 🌐 www.cruzroja.es

> **EMERGENCY NUMBERS**
> **General emergencies** 📞 112 (people who are hard of hearing can fax 900 500 112 or text 679 436 200)
> **Fire brigade** 📞 080

Embassies & consulates

Foreign embassies are in Madrid but some countries also maintain consulates in Barcelona:

Australia 📍 Plaza Gala Placidia 1–3, 1st floor 📞 934 909 013 🌐 www.embaustralia.es

Canada  Elisenda de Pinós 10 932 042 700 www.canada-es.org
Ireland  Gran Via Carlos III 94 934 915 021 www.foreignaffairs.gov.ie
New Zealand  Travesera de Gracia 64 932 090 399
www.nzembassy.com
UK  Avinguda Diagonal 477 933 666 200 www.ukinspain.com
US  Paseo Reina Elisenda de Montcada 23 932 802 227
www.embusa.es

Lost property

You'll have most chance of finding a lost object if you left it by mistake
on a plane, bus or train; contact the company in question and see if it
has been handed in. Otherwise, report the loss of valuable items to a
police station. You have little chance of retrieving them but you will need
an official form to make an insurance claim.

EMERGENCY PHRASES

	Catalan	Spanish
Help!	Auxili!	¡Socorro!
Stop!	Pareu!	¡Pare!
Call a doctor!	Telefoneu un metge!	¡Llame a un médico!
Call an ambulance!	Telefoneu una ambulància!	¡Llame a una ambulancia!
Call the police!	Telefoneu la policia!	¡Llame a la policía!
Call the fire brigade!	Telefoneu els bombers!	¡Llame a los bomberos!
Where's the nearest hospital?	On és l'hospital més proper?	¿Dónde está el hospital más próximo?

GETTING AROUND

Car hire

When hiring a car you will be asked to show your passport and an EU or international driving licence. The major car hire companies have offices at the three airports and in the cities and resorts. You can usually get the best deal by reserving a car from home at the same time as making a flight or holiday booking.

Avis ☎ 902 180 854 ⓦ www.avis.es
Hertz ☎ 902 402 405 ⓦ www.hertz.es

DRIVING RULES & CONDITIONS

The Spanish drive on the right and the highway code is similar to that of other European countries, with internationally recognisable traffic signs. Most national driving licences are valid but it is advisable to have an International Driving Licence.

Seatbelts are obligatory and children under 12 should travel in the back seats. Speed limits are 120 km/h (75 miles/h) on motorways, 100 km/h (60 miles/h) on main roads, 90 km/h (55 miles/h) on other roads and 50 km/h (30 miles/h) in built-up areas. There are two types of motorway in Spain: toll-paying *autopistas* such as the A7 along the coast, and non-toll *autovías*. Maps do not always distinguish clearly between the two but there is always a main-road alternative to a toll road. Petrol (*gasolina*) is available as *super*, *normal* (both leaded), *sin plomo* (unleaded) and *gasoil* (diesel).

The police can issue on-the-spot fines for traffic offences, and being a foreigner does not give you exemption. There are heavy penalties for drinking and driving.

In your car you must carry a red warning triangle, replacement light bulbs, and a reflective jacket in the passenger compartment to wear in case of a road-side emergency.

Buses

The cities and main resorts have efficient networks of local buses. Information is easily available from the relevant tourist office. Longer-distance buses or coaches run from the resorts to almost all the places described in this book. Different bus companies operate different routes, but you can ask for times and details at any tourist information office or bus station. The principal coach stations are at Barcelona, Tarragona and Girona.

Ferries

Various companies operate boat services between the resorts of the Costa Dorada and Costa Brava. Ask for details at the harbour of your resort or in the tourist information office. As well as being a way of getting from A to B, a 'cruise' along the coast can give great views – especially on the Costa Brava – and keep the kids happily occupied.

For ferries from the port of Barcelona to Menorca, Mallorca and Ibiza, contact Acciona Trasmediterránea. ☎ 902 454 645 🌐 www.trasmediterranea.es

Taxis

Taxis are conspicuous, complete with a sign and a green light advertising that they are for hire. They are easily hailed in Barcelona and the other major cities. Alternatively, they can be found at taxi stands outside railway stations and in the main squares. Fares are controlled by meter but there may be surcharges for night, destinations outside the urban area, or for carrying luggage. In small towns taxis are not metered and you should agree the fare in advance.

Trains

There are two train companies in Catalonia:

RENFE (Red Nacional de Ferrocarriles Españoles) Operates mainline and some local trains. ☎ 902 240 202 🌐 www.renfe.es

FGC (Ferrocarrils de la Generalitat de Catalunya) Operates lines around Barcelona and funicular railways. ☎ 932 051 515 🌐 www.fgc.net

HEALTH, SAFETY & CRIME
Health
British citizens, like all EU nationals, are entitled to free treatment from the Spanish social security system on production of a European Health Insurance Card. The EHIC is available free of charge through most UK post offices or through the UK Department of Health (☎ 0845 606 2030 ⓦ www.dh.gov.uk). Many travellers prefer to take out private medical insurance before going to Spain to give them greater choice of healthcare should the worst happen.

Minor health problems can often be cleared up by consulting a *farmacia*, a chemist's shop, which is indicated by a green cross sign. Pharmacists are trained to advise on common ailments. Out of hours, there is always a *farmacia de guardia* open in every neighbourhood; you'll find its address posted in the window of other *farmacias*. *Farmacias* should not be confused with *parafarmacias*, which sell non-prescription medical supplies and where the staff are not qualified to give advice.

Alternatively, you can ask in the tourist information office or town hall of any large international resort for the names of doctors and dentists who speak English.

Safety
Your personal safety is most at risk at beaches. Pay strict attention to beach warning flags. A red flag means it is not safe to swim and it should be respected even if the sea looks calm. In recent years there have been infestations of jellyfish on Catalan beaches; these cause nasty stings.

Crime
The coasts and cities of Catalonia have their share of petty crime but most of it is opportunist and a few simple precautions will make sure you are not an easy target. Watch out for pickpockets in crowded places like markets and bars and wear your bag in front of you. Leave valuables in a hotel safe and never leave anything on display in a parked car.

Catalonia effectively has three police forces. Most conspicuous is the Policía Municipal (Policia Local in Catalan), which is responsible for traffic

problems and low-level policing. The Policía Nacional is in charge of more serious crime. The paramilitary Guardia Civil, meanwhile, takes care of highway patrols and customs. Any of the three will respond to an emergency by contacting the requisite force or other service.

Policía Municipal ☏ 092
Policía Nacional ☏ 091
Guardia Civil ☏ 062

MEDIA

The most popular European and US newspapers, including the *International Herald Tribune*, the *Financial Times* and the *Guardian*, are available from newsstands (*kioskos de prensa*) in all resorts and cities. Many hotels and apartment blocks have satellite TV piped to the rooms with programmes in English.

OPENING HOURS

Banks ⏱ 09.00–13.30 Mon–Fri
Businesses (government and private) ⏱ 09.00–14.00 & 16.00–20.00 Mon–Fri. In summer, some offices may work a reduced day (⏱ 08.00–15.00).
Entertainment centres Larger cinemas have several showings a day between 16.00 and 23.00. Some theatres offer two daily performances at 18.00 and 22.00. Bars for drinking and musical venues open ⏱ 21.00–03.00 and discos 11.30–05.00 or 06.00.
Museums ⏱ 09.00–13.00 & 16.00–20.00 Tues–Sat, 09.00–12.00 or 13.00 Sun. Larger museums have continuous opening hours without a lunch break. Although most museums close on Mondays, there are exceptions, and the tourist office in Barcelona issues a list of these.
Post offices ⏱ 09.00–14.00 Mon–Fri, 09.00–13.00 Sat
Restaurants See Food & drink, page 92.
Shops ⏱ 09.00 or 10.00–13.30 & 17.00–20.00 (or maybe a little later) Mon–Sat. In the summer some shops open later in the afternoon when the heat starts to die down and stay open correspondingly later. In small towns you may find the shops closed on a Saturday afternoon.

Department stores and other large shops are open continuously 10.00–21.00. Shops are generally closed on Sundays except on special occasions such as the run-up to Christmas. Markets start around 08.00 or earlier and are usually closed by 14.00.

RELIGION

Spain is a predominantly Catholic country. There are very few Protestants and only a small Jewish community. The proportion of Muslims is increasing mainly due to immigration from North Africa.

SMOKING

Smoking is banned in public areas of buildings in Spain. Large bars and restaurants are permitted to designate a smoking area. Small bars can choose to be smoking or non-smoking as long as they are clearly labelled. Some hotels are entirely non-smoking; others offer rooms set aside for non-smokers.

● *Pretty street sign in Tossa*

TIME DIFFERENCES

Spain is on Central European Time (CET). During Daylight Saving Time (late Mar–late Sept), the clocks are put ahead one hour. At 12.00 in Spain in summer, times elsewhere are as follows:

Australia Eastern Standard Time 20.00, Central Standard Time 19.30, Western Standard Time 18.00

New Zealand 22.00

South Africa 12.00

UK 11.00

USA and **Canada** Newfoundland Time 07.30, Atlantic Canada Time 07.00, Eastern Time 06.00, Central Time 05.00, Mountain Time 04.00, Pacific Time 03.00, Alaska 02.00

TIPPING

There are no fixed rules on tipping nor is a tip ever expected. In bars and restaurants it is customary to round the bill up to the nearest euro, leaving a few coins on the table.

TOILETS

There are few public toilets in Spain. If there isn't one within range, the best bet is to go into a bar (but it's polite to order a drink). Shopping centres and department stores also have toilets for the use of customers. Ask for *los servicios*.

TRAVELLERS WITH DISABILITIES

Spain has few facilities for travellers with disabilities but the situation is slowly improving. More information is available from the following:

COCEMFE (Spanish Association for the Physically and Mentally Handicapped) ⓐ Luis Cabrera 63, Madrid ⓣ 917 443 600
ⓦ www.cocemfe.es

RADAR (Royal Association for Disability and Rehabilitation)
ⓣ UK 0207 250 3222 ⓦ www.radar.org.uk

Holiday Care Service ⓣ UK 0845 124 9971
ⓦ www.holidaycare.org.uk